Through Many Lives

A TALE OF TIME TRAVEL THROUGH THE YUGAS

by Nayaswami Savitri Simpson

ISBN: 978-1-56589-265-1
ePub: 978-1-56589-509-6

Printed in the United States of America

This novel is dedicated to my spiritual teacher

Swami Kriyananda

His wisdom and the lyrics to his beautiful songs appear throughout the book.

Acknowledgements

Through Many Lives was lovingly edited by Anandi Cornell, and proofread by Prakash Van Cleave, Leah Kirk, and Lakshman Heubert. The yuga dates were corrected and clarified by Byasa Steinmetz. Many great suggestions were given to the author by Sudarshan Simpson and Joseph (Purushottama) Selbie. The cover artwork was created by Cris Crisman and Ashleigh Moore. Many thanks to all!

INTRODUCTION: WHAT IS A YUGA?

Yuga is a Sanskrit word which means an epoch, long eras, or eons of time.

In India, and particularly in the teachings of yoga, time is described as moving through cycles, rather than in a linear fashion. The yuga theory explains that there have been in the past, and will be in the future, both "higher" and "lower" ages, manifesting in cyclic patterns.

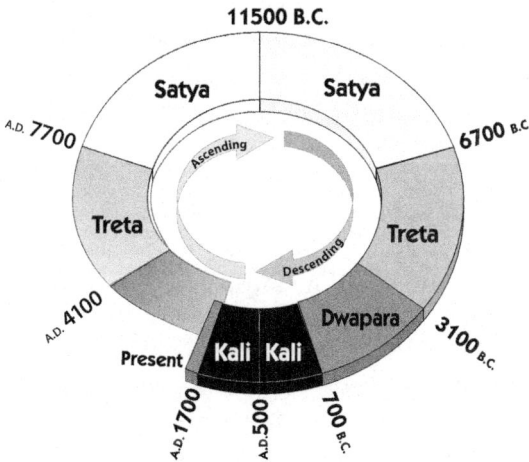

Just as our planet's seasons move through summer, autumn, winter, and spring, each yuga involves stages of gradual change, through which the earth and the consciousness of human beings, as a whole, progress or regress.

Toward the end of the 19th century, a man with exceptional credentials as a scholar wrote a book called *The Holy Science*. Swami Sri Yukteswar (1855–1936), of Serampore, Bengal, was a master of great wisdom, deeply learned in the ancient lore of India. In his book he stated that, according to a system of chronology that was established by astronomers in ancient times, our planet moves through great cycles of time called yugas.

The Holy Science appeared in 1894. In it Sri Yukteswar described this ancient chronology in detail, and corrected certain misinterpretations of that chronology that had crept in over recent centuries.

Long ago in India and in other very old civilizations, different names were given for four ages. The Egyptians called them the ages of gods, demi-gods, heroes, and men. The Greeks named them the golden, silver, bronze, and iron ages.

The ages described in the yuga theory are four: *Satya Yuga*, the spiritual age; *Treta Yuga*, the mental age; *Dwapara Yuga*, the energy age; and *Kali Yuga*, the dark or materially oriented age. *Kali Yuga* was said to be an age of spiritual ignorance.

Sri Yukteswar announced that the world had actually left the lowest age of Kali Yuga recently and entered the next and higher age of Dwapara Yuga. And he was able to give these teachings modern, scientific support.

According to Sri Yukteswar, a full yuga cycle takes 24,000 years to complete, and includes two divisions: 12,000 years of *ascending* consciousness and 12,000 years of *descending* consciousness.

Looking at this system scientifically, from an astronomer's point of view, the first division of the cycle of the yugas represents a progression from the time when our solar system is the farthest from the center of our galaxy to the time when it is closest to that center.

The explanation given for the progression of the yugas is that our sun has a dual star, and that these two stars revolve around each other. Because of this revolution, our sun with its planets moves in a great elliptical orbit toward, then away from, the center of our galaxy, which is a tremendous vortex of energy.

The yogic teachings say that rays of spiritual energy pour out from the galactic center, and that the closer our solar system comes to this center, the more energy floods our planet. As the level of energy increases, human consciousness becomes correspondingly more enlightened and aware.

As our solar system moves away from the source of these energy rays, human consciousness becomes duller, that is, less able to understand things as they truly are. Spiritual progress becomes much more difficult.

Our solar system reached the point farthest away from the galactic center in roughly 500 AD, during the heart of the Dark Age, or Kali Yuga.

We are now moving back again toward the galactic center; consequently, people are more able to understand the more subtle truths of life. They have begun to recognize, for example, that matter is not essentially solid, but is really energy. In fact, it is only because we've moved into the more enlightened age of Ascending Dwapara Yuga that mankind is able to understand the concept of the yuga cycle.

The two lower yugas in this cycle are Dwapara Yuga, "The Age of Energy," and Kali Yuga, "The Material Age."

In 1900 AD our planet entered fully into Ascending Dwapara Yuga, and it has been amazing to see how much, in just one century, we have advanced. Everything we know of modern times — airplanes, cars, electronics, radios, television, computers — started after 1900. And we're just at the beginning of this new "Age of Energy." The discoveries that lie ahead of us are enormous, and all will be based on an awareness of energy as the underlying reality of matter.

A very different kind of world and universe will open up as we advance into this new era. Before the end of Ascending Dwapara Yuga in 4100 AD, we will have learned to bypass the limitations of the speed of light, and will conquer the delusion of space and distance; we will realize that the most distant galaxy is as easy to visit as are our present surroundings.

The two higher ages are Treta Yuga, "The Mental Age," and Satya Yuga, "The Spiritual Age."

Beginning in 4100 AD (Ascending Treta Yuga), people will understand that consciousness engenders energy and that with their own minds they can direct energy to accomplish their goals. As mankind's mental control, intuition, and knowledge of the universe evolve, mental telepathy will occur naturally. This understanding will be the hallmark of Treta Yuga.

Treta Yuga will also be an age marked by people's ability to overcome all limitations of time. In Treta Yuga, most people will understand that time, like space, is a delusion, and that the most ancient civilizations exist, not in the distant past, but right now, in the eternal present.

This novel, *Through Many Lives: A Tale of Time Travel Through the Yugas,* begins in Treta Yuga in 5910 AD, about 3,900 years from the present time. Because of the ability to overcome many of the limitations of time in Treta Yuga, the characters in this novel are able to visit different yugas, going thousands of years into the past or the future.

In a certain sense, it does not matter which yuga we find ourselves in on this earth or on any other planet (Paramhansa Yogananda said there are many inhabited planets). For as we reincarnate from life to life, through *many* lifetimes, the best way to live is to tune in to the higher octave of the time in which we find ourselves, and to use it for our own, and all others' highest possible good.

The yoga sciences teach that the goal of life is Self-realization and oneness with all that is. That goal is possible for us during any lifetime and in any yuga.

If you would like to learn more details about the yuga theory — its explanation of the history of our planet and its interesting ways of predicting the future — we highly recommend *The Yugas*, by Joseph Selbie and David Steinmetz, published by Crystal Clarity Publishers, www.crystalclarity.com. This is, without question, the best book ever written on the subject.

As you read this novel, I hope you *will* become interested in learning more about the endlessly fascinating topic of the yugas — and of course that you will be well-entertained by the story and its characters. I am glad to receive comments or questions: savitri@ananda.org.

In friendship,
Nayaswami Savitri Simpson

Ananda Village, California, USA
311 Ascending Dwapara Yuga
(December, 2011 AD)

The yuga diagram and information about the yugas is taken, in part, and with thanks, from the article, "The Higher Yugas and the Unfolding of Human Potential," by Swami Kriyananda, in Ananda Sangha's *Clarity Magazine* (Fall, 2010).

CHAPTER 1

Time does not go as people think, in a straight line
from past to future.
Rather it proceeds in a circle around a center
in the eternal NOW.
Time is, basically, an illusion.
Whatever was in the past not only <u>was</u>,
but is now, and will be, forever.

— Swami Kriyananda

5910 AD (1810, ASCENDING TRETA YUGA)

Simeon's hair and eyes were his most unusual features. He had very long, slightly curly hair that fell almost to his waist — silvery-white in color — appropriate for someone over 200 years old. His sparkling eyes almost matched his hair; they were unfathomable in their depth, and radiant with internal light. Looking deeply into his eyes was like looking into infinity.

I felt a shiver of anticipation when he spoke. "You have dedicated many hours every day to deepening your meditation and strengthening your inner life. This process will serve you well in the years to come. Traveling through time can cause a spiritually weak person to become confused."

Barely able to conceal my eagerness I said, "I'm ready? I'm ready to travel through time?"

He looked calmly at me and nodded.

———

Thomas woke from his dream with a joyful thrill. Could it be true? This dream seemed so much more vivid and filled with clear color and light than a regular dream. Was it a premonition?

"Patience!" he warned himself. "Simeon always tells us to

1

be calm and wait for the answers to be revealed at the right time. I'll wait calmly to see if my dream was based in truth."

Later that day, Simeon was leaning comfortably against a granite boulder near the river that ran near Thomas's small home. Simeon had just sent a mental message to Thomas to join him there. Now he waited patiently, enjoying the warmth of the late afternoon sunshine and the gentle river sounds.

"Sir, I'm on my way to join you by the river!" Thomas sent a joyful thought to his teacher. "Mind-speak" was an easy way to communicate. In Treta Yuga, it was just about the *only* way people talked to each other. Lapses into oral communication usually meant the speaker was upset, overly excited, or unable to concentrate for some reason.

Simeon had taught in the Halls of Wisdom for more than a hundred years and was very much loved by students past and present. Because he rarely paid personal visits to his students, Thomas was overjoyed at this invitation. Perhaps the surprise visit had something to do with his dream.

Handsome and strong, Thomas was a young man of sixty. He was average in height for Treta Yuga, about eight feet tall, intellectually brilliant, and very kind. He had been a student in the Halls of Wisdom for many years, most recently in a small seminar of advanced students led by Simeon.

Thomas had grown to love Simeon very much. His calm wisdom was the hallmark of a life dedicated to spiritual pursuits and to the careful instruction of young people. "Simeon!" Thomas grasped his teacher's outstretched hands and gazed into his sparkling eyes. "To what do I owe the honor of your visit? Would you like to come back to my home for some refreshments?"

"No, I'm content to remain here, Thomas. You know how much I enjoy nature's beauty. But thank you for your kind invitation. Sit beside me here. Let's meditate for a while." Eagerly Thomas joined his teacher. Together they sat in deep stillness and harmony, communing inwardly. Though Thomas had often been overwhelmed by the power of Simeon's love and blessings, these feelings were even greater today — they felt somehow "amplified." His meditation was blissful!

Feeling timeless, Thomas wondered how long they had meditated. When he opened his eyes, it was just after sunset. A full moon had risen in the eastern skies. Simeon said quietly to Thomas, "My son, thank you for meditating with me here by the river. We need to discuss something that I know has long been on your mind."

"Time travel?" asked Thomas in a whisper-thought.

Simeon nodded and smiled in reply. "Yes. I know about your dream last night. It predicted your immediate future correctly. We need to discuss this in depth. During tomorrow's seminar, I'll begin to instruct you and your fellow students on the subject of time travel.

"But before making the general announcement to the whole class, I wanted to speak with you privately. I have been happy with your progress in all of your studies. But more importantly, I have watched your spiritual endeavors — and I am very pleased with what you have achieved.

"You have dedicated many hours every day to deepening your meditation and to strengthening your inner life. This process will serve you well in the years to come. Traveling through time can cause a spiritually weak person to become confused."

Thomas was amazed that Simeon repeated the very words he'd said in the dream!

"Thank you, Sir. I'm honored that you've come to tell me this. I'll do my best to live up to the high ideals you've set for us, no matter where (or when!) I may be." Thomas did not try to hide his smile of delight, nor did Simeon mind his student's enormous enthusiasm for what was to come.

Joining in Thomas's celebratory mood, Simeon said, "It's a warm night! Let's go for a swim in the river!" What a special evening! Teacher and student laughed and played together like children. Afterward, they walked along the riverside path, under the bright moon and stars, discussing grand, cosmic theories about the nature of time.

As he was leaving, Simeon sent these parting thoughts to Thomas: "Time is a deep, cosmic secret. No one truly knows what it means. Let us explore this mystery together."

CHAPTER 2

"You can't change history, but history can change you."

— Swami Kriyananda

Thomas arrived in the Halls of Wisdom a few minutes early and attempted to settle his mind before class. He expected Simeon at any moment.

His studies with Simeon were the highlight of his life. Thomas had never met anyone so wise. Simeon's was a wisdom born of intuition and spiritual depth. Truth flowed through him effortlessly, with clarity, grace, and power. Thomas could not help but feel awe in his presence. And yet he always felt deeply and unconditionally loved by Simeon.

Thomas was a Fourth Level student in the Halls of Wisdom, but none of the students knew how many levels there were nor how long their study would last. Though other students speculated on this subject often, Thomas simply felt grateful to be here and thrilled at the vast wisdom to be gained.

"Thomas!" Jarred from his musing by a very loud voice, Thomas greeted his friend and fellow classmate Sabella. She continued loudly, "What do you think we'll study today in class? Simeon hinted in our last session that it's time for us to get into something a little more challenging. What do you think that would be?" Sabella then continued to reel off possibilities at a rapid pace.

Thomas looked away from Sabella and thought (privately): "Sabella is a very nice person! Sweet, kind, and sort of pretty. But she thinks too much and too fast! She insists on speaking loudly to me with her *voice*. Why doesn't she use the thought transmission we learned together, many years ago?"

Immediately Simeon's words rang through his mind: "Thomas, what you criticize in another person may well be a fault in you." Simeon had arrived in the classroom and also in Thomas's mental pathways.

Thomas's thoughts were never shielded from Simeon. He didn't want them to be! For how else could he truly learn from this wisest of beings? He turned to see Simeon entering their learning zone and piercing Thomas with his radiant eyes. There was a twinkle in his eyes today and a slight smile on his lips.

"Thank you, Simeon, for monitoring my thoughts. You're right. I do think too much and often verbalize when I should be mentally broadcasting. But don't you think Sabella speaks out excessively?"

"Her behavior is not your concern." Simeon thought back, this time with a mental chuckle. "Your primary mission is to change yourself. We've been over those grounds a time or two before, haven't we?"

"Yes, that is very true," Thomas inwardly admitted to himself and to his teacher. One of his first courses with Simeon had been on how to behave correctly at all times — both inwardly and outwardly. And he was still working on those lessons. Would he never perfect them? But he was happy that Simeon never let up on the mental course corrections. He shared his teacher's goal of perfection.

As Simeon began to interact with the other students, Thomas sat back in his chair and gazed lovingly at his teacher, appreciating as always Simeon's unique appearance. He was just a bit shorter than Thomas, about 7 feet 6 inches tall. He was well proportioned, strong and fit, though Thomas had never seen or heard of him exercising in order to keep himself that way.

Sometimes his silver hair seemed silky and lighter than air, floating around his head, defying the law of gravity. His skin was generally dark with a slightly blue-violet cast to it, though his skin tone could look lighter or darker at different times. He wore simple clothes, always in a bright royal blue color. He seemed to prefer lightweight, flowing fabrics, but no matter what he wore — and even in his most playful or casual moments — he looked imposing and dignified.

Simeon spent most of his time in the Halls of Wisdom,

teaching and counseling students. If he had a private life, he never spoke of it.

One of the most remarkable things about Simeon was that his physical appearance seemed to shift daily or even hourly, depending on whom he was with or what was going on around him. Thomas often wondered if Simeon's vibratory levels changed to match the vibrations of his surroundings or of the people he was with.

Simeon was not married, nor had he mentioned ever having had a wife. Admired, respected, and even sometimes a little feared, he walked through the world alone, yet he never seemed lonely. Centered and deeply at peace, he seemed always complete in himself.

Simeon could be riotously funny, putting everyone at ease and bringing any subject matter to life with humorous stories or exciting tales to illustrate various points. His former students love to recount some of his memorable classes — the life lessons were indelibly etched in their memories.

Each one of his students loved and respected him, considering him a personal friend and refuge in times of uncertainty. Never one to coddle them in their weak times, Simeon seemed effortlessly to lift them to be their very best selves. It was impossible to be negative or depressed around Simeon.

"How does he do that?" Thomas often wondered, and, "Will *I* ever be able to help others in that way?"

Silence settled over their learning zone as Simeon and all the students sat on colorful pillows scattered about the soft grass. Simeon began each class with long, deep meditation. He often told them that meditation was the most important part of their classes.

Four hours passed without physical movement or mental flutter among the students. They had grown to love the meditation sessions that preceded their classes. Simeon ended the meditation with beautiful music. He softly sang an ancient song to them, to lead them gently out of their meditative state:

Where He dwells, the earth in gladness
  Puts forth sweet herbs, shading trees.
Gay streams bound through summer meadows;
  Fragrance blows on ev'ry breeze.
They with happiness are blessed
Who the Lord have made their guest.°

After a brief discussion of today's meditation session, Simeon announced a break. Students stretched, went to the spring for a cool drink, and snacked on delicious fresh fruits. In a short time, Simeon's mental call gathered them together again.

He looked at their eager, smiling faces and knew they suspected something special was coming today. Of course, Thomas was already "in the know." Simeon inwardly commended Thomas for keeping their discussion to himself.

"I believe that by now we have sufficiently covered the subject of the great planetary cycles of time. Are there any questions or comments about the yugas before we proceed?" As usual, Simeon was speaking to them through their minds.

"Do the past and future always resemble each other exactly?" A student named Darien thought this question to Simeon. "For example, if we time-traveled back to the date in Descending Treta Yuga that corresponds exactly to our current date here in Ascending Treta Yuga, would everything look and feel just the same to us?"

"Excellent question, Darien! I think you must have been reading my mind (general chuckles all around) about our subject for today, because it may answer this question for you in a dramatic way. And that subject is. . . ." Here Simeon paused and lifted his eyebrows, mentally asking his students to speculate.

"Time travel!" several of them said together — Sabella, once again forgetting to think instead of say it, answered loudly. Simeon smiled at her as she lowered her head and blushed.

"Yes, time travel."

Excitement filled the room. Though not surprised by the

announcement, Thomas was happily caught up in the universal exuberance. History had always been his favorite subject. He thrilled to think about the idea of actually traveling back into historical times, instead of simply reading about them. He tried not to be excessively excited about time travel, but Simeon knew. . . . Simeon always knew.

CHAPTER 3

"Thomas, why would you like to travel through time, and what makes it possible for *some people* to do so?"

Thomas did not miss the emphasis on the words "some people" and knew he must calm his mind and make it receptive to what Simeon wanted to teach them today. He desperately wanted to be one of those "some people" — the sooner, the better.

"Sir, you know of my great interest in history. Being there would surely be better than just speculating about historical events. There must be *much* to learn from the past mistakes of ancient civilizations — so that we do not make the same mistakes again."

"Ah, the beautiful optimism of the young," thought Simeon to himself, this time shielding his thoughts from all. "Do we really learn from the past? If history has taught us anything, it's that human beings and civilizations seem determined to make the same mistakes again and again."

Thomas continued, "As for what makes time travel possible, I assume you are going to show us. I have talked to others who have done it, but they would only say, 'Your teacher will help you when the time is right.'"

Simeon remained silent, which made Thomas think he wanted him to continue.

"Sir, I think that time travel must be something like what we learned in our courses on non-mechanical space travel or basic teleportation skills. We must somehow use our minds to transport our bodies somewhere else, or in this case 'some-when' else."

Simeon smiled. "Yes, there are some similarities, but there are also some very important differences and laws you must fully understand before you travel in time."

Aloud Thomas blurted: "Yes! You wouldn't want to go back

in time and kill your great grandfather, because then you wouldn't be here now, right?"

"Perhaps a good idea in your case," thought Loralon, who didn't particularly like Thomas. He tried to keep his thoughts on this matter shielded from everybody, but he didn't do a very good job of it. Though as bright and accomplished as the rest of his classmates, Loralon envied the special attention Simeon gave Thomas. Now Loralon received a strong glance from Simeon and from a few others in the class, too — letting him know his shielding skills were not successful.

"Sorry about that!" he thought.

Fortunately, Thomas had not noticed the exchange and waited to hear how Simeon would reply to him.

Simeon told them, "Please understand that our ability to travel into the past does not include the ability to *change* the past. You will observe and, to some degree, feel that you are participating in what is going on around you.

"But you are not truly *there* in the sense Thomas is mentioning. This 'what-if-you-kill-your-great-great-grandfather conundrum' has been a question for anyone who's ever contemplated time travel. I'm glad that Thomas brought it up, and we will certainly address that issue later.

"But first, Darien, I have not forgotten your question about Treta Yuga. If you travel back to a time that is comparable to where you are now, except that you are 12,000 years in the past and therefore in Descending Treta Yuga instead of Ascending Treta Yuga, you will find that the environment and people are not as they are now. Would anyone like to comment on why this might be?"

Loralon, hoping to reestablish himself in the good graces of his teacher and classmates, offered an answer: "Sir, I think things would be at least slightly different simply because people's knowledge levels, consciousness, and sense of *dharma* (right action) would be moving in a downward direction, rather than toward a higher one, as is happening now in Ascending Treta Yuga. This difference would surely influence people's lives in many ways."

As he thought, "Loralon is right," Simeon beamed him love. Loralon basked in that love and felt his heart soothed and calmed. At such moments, he forgot his jealousy of Thomas and simply loved everybody equally, for ". . . are not we all one in the Spirit?" He wished it weren't so easy for him to forget the basic teaching of the ages.

Thomas could tell something important was happening between Simeon and Loralon — one of those moments that occurred frequently in their seminars, when someone received a thought-message from Simeon particular to that one alone.

Though he had experienced many such moments himself, Thomas now felt simply impatient to move forward with their time-travel studies.

"Patience, Thomas!" he heard in his head. Sigh. Would he ever learn to keep himself in that calm, steady frame of mind that Simeon seemed to have at all times?

"Yes, you will," was the answer from Simeon, directed to Thomas only. "You have this quality within you already. It is who and what you really are in your divine nature. You just need to fully realize it." With this kind reminder from his teacher, Thomas felt blessed and uplifted.

"Now, class, it's time to begin your Level Five studies in time travel: how it works and exactly how to do it — especially since I see you all are so un-anxious to begin." Simeon laughed at their amazement in being promoted from Level Four to Level Five with no fuss or praise.

"One of the hallmarks of Treta Yuga is the annihilation of time and space. You have experienced traveling to other planets and stars in this vast material universe. What did you learn from being able to go wherever you wished instantaneously?"

They thought in unison, "No matter where you go, there you are!"

"Correct!" and all laughed heartily. Simeon had emphasized this principle frequently.

"Wherever you go you take yourself with you." Simeon grew serious now. "This is just as true with traveling through time. What else did you learn as you traveled through space?"

"That the material universe is a very big place, almost beyond comprehension, and very diverse in its manifestations," thought Vilma, one of the quietest of Simeon's students.

"And yet. . . ," Simeon prompted her.

". . . and yet, the similarities among all creatures in the universe are greater than their differences, for the consciousness of all beings is part of the Consciousness of their Creator."

"Yes," Simeon thought to himself with deep satisfaction. "I do believe they are ready for a next step in their training."

For the rest of the day's session Simeon outlined the history of time travel in Treta Yuga and how the laws of time travel were rediscovered early in Ascending Treta Yuga — sharing what their ancestors had learned from time travel, the mistakes they'd made, and how they'd learned to correct those mistakes.

Some of these tales were mind-boggling, others funny, but all were instructive and fascinating to the students. Simeon projected his thoughts in the form of small movies in their minds. The students attuned so deeply with his thoughts and word-pictures that it became difficult to feel where his mind ended and theirs began.

But now Simeon sensed they'd received enough knowledge for one session. Though they begged him not to stop, he paid no attention. He knew that more information would overwhelm their ability to absorb what they were learning. No assignments were given today, except the usual one to meditate deeply before sleep and let the knowledge of the day be realized as intuitive wisdom.

CHAPTER 4

After saying goodnight to his instructor and classmates, Thomas wandered alone toward the park, as he often did after Simeon's classes. He strolled along the creek that flowed into the river close to his home. The Halls of Wisdom builders had chosen this idyllic natural setting to allow students a quiet place for reflecting on their lessons.

Thomas sat in his favorite spot beside the sparkling river. The air was fresh and the river sounds were soft and soothing. He dangled his bare feet in the cool water.

Today the river seemed to have special meaning for him, somehow seeming to represent time itself. He watched, heard, and felt the river flow by him, touching him, but not being touched by him. He felt the power of its natural force and sensed its message to him about time, about time travel, about life in general. Another of the ancient songs that Simeon often sang for them came into his mind:

> Life flows on like a river
>   That homes to the sea:
> One hour bounding through mountain vales;
>   One hour, winding through a lea.
> None may linger on the way:
> None may coax time to stay!
> Fleeting scenes move by us like a dream:
> Cling not: None will be your own.
> Lest you grieve to be alone,
> Go within you: There's your home!©

The words and melody were simple and he sang them to the river several times. The river seemed to sing back to him in its own lovely way. Tears sprang to his eyes — tears both of joy *and* sadness. One line in the song affected him deeply: "Lest you grieve to be alone. . . ."

Thomas *was* alone in this world. Though he had many friends and the great blessing of his teacher, he had no family left now except for his younger sister, Alia, who lived on a distant planet. The rest of his family had been killed in the Great Mantric World War III.

He had been spared. Thomas's father had taken him to Simeon and begged him to protect his youngest son through those dark days. Simeon managed to save Thomas and many other orphaned children during that time. Simeon was, in a way, a beloved father figure, as well as teacher, to Thomas.

Thomas had very little memory of his parents or siblings. In his limited memory, his mother was a cloud of golden hair bending over him, singing forgotten words of love; his father was two strong arms, lifting him high into the air. He remembered his father praying for his safety. His brothers and sisters were blurs of laughter and play. No other memories of them remained. Perhaps he could go back in time and meet them again. As soon as he had that thought, he sensed this return would never happen. Why not? He must ask Simeon about it. For now, he struggled to overcome his sadness as he sat alone, yearning — for whom or what he could not say.

With blond hair and greenish-blue eyes, Thomas, at the age of 60, was a handsome and well-built young man. Because the natural life expectancy in Treta Yuga was about 300 years, many of Thomas's friends were now finding partners and thinking of marriage and children.

Maybe what troubled him now was the "urge to merge," as Simeon laughingly called it. Thomas had experienced some relationships that went beyond simple friendship, but for now his studies came first. Though he longed for something, he also didn't feel ready to divide his energies with a serious love relationship.

An expert swimmer, Thomas decided that his twinges of loneliness should be "washed away" by a long swim. Removing his simple tunic, he walked into the cool river, shivered a bit until he got used to it, then plunged into the crystal stream, and began to swim underwater. In this quiet world of joyful light and color, he felt both invigorated and calmed. The mood vanished as if it had never been. He swam two miles and returned to the riverbank to dry off in the waning sunlight. He put on his tunic and walked slowly home.

As he walked through the darkening shadows, he sang softly:

Life is a dream.
Time, like a stream,
Carries our burdens away. . . .©

He thought of the many beautiful songs Simeon had taught them over the years. Old as the songs often were, they came unbidden into his heart and mind, at just the right moments in his life, gently reminding him of needed lessons. These thoughts reminded Thomas that he was giving voice lessons tomorrow afternoon and needed to prepare his mental notes before then.

Students in the Halls of Wisdom did not attend classes daily, but alternated study with service to others in a way suited to their natural gifts. Thomas had been recognized as a "teacher type" early in his years there, and thus spent every other day teaching in the lower levels of learning. Others might spend those days on landscaping, childcare, or some other area that resonated with their natural aptitude.

Ascending Treta Yuga society operated without salaries or other forms of monetary exchange. Each person was expected to give energy in equal measure to what he or she received.

Thomas enjoyed teaching and was good at it. He usually taught simple physical skills like swimming, skiing, and yoga postures. He also taught voice and instrumental music, as well as basic meditation techniques. Occasionally, if there was a need, he taught the young children subjects such as telekinesis and color/sound healing techniques.

He especially enjoyed teaching music. Music was a beautiful language, one which Thomas knew well. He composed music and guided his students to do so also. He and his students frequently presented concerts in the Halls of Wisdom.

Sometimes his students joined other teachers' classes for their performances. Particularly enjoyable for him were concerts with Sabella and her students. Whatever he thought about Sabella's boisterousness in Simeon's seminars, he had to admit that she had truly mastered teaching the subtle art of *photism*.

Photism is the ability to see a sound or to hear a color. At these special concerts, anticipated and enjoyed by hundreds of people, music was played and sung, and also projected into the environment and into the minds of the audience in the form of shapes and colors. Each musical note has a corresponding vibration on the color spectrum. The shade and intensity of the color depend on the octave and volume in which the note is sung or played.

Shapes also sprang from the vibrations of the music, forming themselves into abstractions or actual scenes, according to the type of music being performed.

Such concerts were enthralling, and were always presented to capacity crowds.

The music that Thomas directed, presented, and sometimes even composed was very inspiring, but he knew that Sabella's God-given talent created an entirely different level of audience enjoyment. Her attunement and creativity with photism were impressive to all who knew her. She was rapidly becoming world famous for her work.

Thomas hoped fame wouldn't go to her head. So far she seemed oblivious to anything other than the joy of the creative process and the happiness it brought to performers and audiences alike. Who knew what her future would bring?

CHAPTER 5

When their class met again, Simeon wasted no time in moving his students into a Level Five time-travel skills workshop and discussing their many questions and concerns.

One of their primary concerns was voiced immediately by Vilma, who was less adventurous than her classmates. "Sir, is it possible to travel back in time and then get stuck there?"

Simeon smiled and explained, "Until you become completely adept at time travel, I, as your guide and instructor, will carefully monitor when and where you go and how long you stay there. Believe me — you'll be back here on schedule!"

Vilma continued, "If we are visiting another era for, say, six months, would six months also pass back in our 'home time'?"

"We will decide beforehand exactly how long you will be in another time frame," Simeon explained.

"We can also determine how much time will *seem* to have passed here while you are in the different time zone. In the early days of experimentation with time travel, it was found to be too stressful for a person to spend six months in another time and return very quickly — say a minute or two after 'leaving.' Through trial and error, it was determined that a ratio of about one day here for each month away is optimal for a smooth transition that is not shocking to one's body or emotions."

Vilma was looking a little pale at this news and thought to Simeon, "So it sounds as though there might be some danger, or at least stress, involved in time travel?"

"Travel to the past involves no risks when you are guided and protected by those who know what they are doing. As for stressful situations, well, life is stressful, no matter where or when you are living. You will experience life in different yugas. Some of these times and places will be so different from what you are used to that you may find them shocking.

That is why we will prepare you carefully before you travel and then spend as much time as needed in debriefing you after your return."

"Er-ah, Sir," thought Luwiten, the youngest class member, who rarely spoke in class. "Perhaps this is a foolish question, but I'm not sure I understand. Do our bodies stay here or go with us to the place and time to which we travel?"

Simeon frowned a bit. "Forgive me for not making this clear. Time travel is done mentally. Your body stays here and now and will be inert, as though in a deep sleep — carefully guarded during the time you are away. When you first begin to time travel, your mind will not know that your body has remained here, in the present time and place. You will be convinced that you are wherever and whenever you have chosen to visit.

In the beginning I will guide you carefully there and back. Later, you will be able to time travel alone, but that is going to be. . . *later*. There is much to learn from the actual experiences you will have, and obviously we want you always to remain safe and calm."

Luwiten, very engaged now, thought carefully, "Could there be a danger of being killed in our travel?"

"No! And can you imagine why not?" Simeon was glad for this question because he was sure it was shared by many in the group.

Thomas, who had stayed quiet as long as possible, felt it was time for him to speak. "Sir, it must be because the past is over and done with. What has happened is fixed and cannot be changed. Even if we 'die' in that particular part of the incarnation, we are only observing. Observing the past would not have an effect on us in this present incarnation."

"Yes, that is right."

Luwiten was not finished with his questions. "But what if, hypothetically speaking, we were to experience death or injury while in the past — wouldn't that somehow traumatize our bodies or minds here in the present?"

"What do you think?" Simeon was quick to evoke thoughtful reactions from his students, rather than simply giving them the answers.

"I don't think I could be completely unaffected by death or injury in the past or at any other time!" said Sabella, once again forgetting to think it instead of say it.

Thomas couldn't resist answering her, "Sabella, surely you understand that you have died many times before. You would be 'there' in the past only mentally, not physically — isn't this so, Simeon? Your body in the present would not die or suffer, so what would be the problem? I think it might be a very educational experience!"

Simeon smiled and winked. "Perhaps that could be arranged especially for you, Thomas (several of his fellow students snickered mentally), but definitely not during your first trip to the past. You are a brave person, but it is enough to deal with finding yourself in another body, time, and place. You don't need more than that for your first experience."

Thomas was listening carefully and wondering about the idea of being in "another body." "Will we be invisible and unnoticed, or will we inhabit somebody's body in the past? Whose body?" He wondered.

"Your own body, of course," answered Simeon. "That is, the body you had when you were alive in that time frame."

After a moment of silence while the students digested his words, Vilma asked quietly, "Sir, does that mean that we are *only* going to go back into times in which we've lived before — that is, into our past lives?"

"You are right, Vilma," Simeon said. "The best way to begin developing your time-travel skills is in the times in which you have lived previously, for these will most strongly attract you. Also, they will be the most interesting for you to observe and to learn from; these lives may seem vaguely familiar or comfortable to you, even though the intervening lifetimes have taken away your memories of them. The difference now will be that when you return from your journey, you will clearly remember everything that happened. There are other ways to travel through time, but for now, this is the mode we will use."

Before Simeon could begin to explain this process more carefully, Loralon had a few more questions: "Will we travel as a group, as we have done when visiting other planets, or will we experience time travel individually?"

"Individually," was the simple reply.

Another question, still not answered to Loralon's satisfaction: "What about the theory of 'In killing your own grandfather, you would eliminate the possibility of your being born in the future'? What effect will our presence in the past have on the future, if any? How can we avoid doing the wrong thing while back there?"

"You must expand your mind to embrace some unusual concepts about the way we have learned to time travel. You will not really be *doing* anything while there. You will be re-living the past as you actually experienced it when it was happening. So there is nothing you will *do* differently from what has already happened. The past is over — frozen, so to speak. But while there, you will not think this is so. You will feel that you have free will, and you will make decisions accordingly. It's just that what you did then is done and cannot be re-done."

"So what's the point of doing this?" The same thought came to Simeon from most of the students.

"It will be extremely educational for you to see what the different eras are like, firsthand. You will see and feel Descending Kali Yuga or Ascending Dwapara Yuga. It will be as real to you as it was when you actually experienced it. And when you return to this time frame, you will have perfect recollection of all you felt and thought.

"It will feel just as though you were traveling through space rather than time, and you will realize that you have the same memories of your life as you had at the time. You will grow stronger in yourself through experiencing parts of your past lives as you actually lived them in different yugas and locations." Simeon's thought-words rang through his students with powerful authority.

Darien now asked, "Sir, will we go farther backward or forward in time than this present 24,000-year yuga cycle? We have learned that our Earth has already passed through thousands of such yuga cycles."

"Good question," Simeon said. "It would be possible to do so, but we've found that it's best to limit students' travels to this particular 24,000-year cycle. Why might this be?"

Thomas answered, "Would it be, Sir, that in the beginning, we need familiarity with the time and place we are visiting, at least to some degree? Time traveling itself may be unusual enough, without traveling outside our present yuga cycle. And 24,000 years should offer plenty of lifetimes to experience without having to go too far back in time. Perhaps, for the same reasons, we won't visit our past lives on other planets, ones that are going through entirely different cycles of time."

Simeon smiled with pleasure at Thomas's grasp of the subject. "Yes, you are correct, both about why we will visit lifetimes which have occurred in our present yuga cycle and why we confine our visits to past lives lived on our home planet."

Sabella asked for a time-out, and Simeon knew she was right. They all needed to move about and relax a little.

During the break, Thomas went to a nearby meadow and did a headstand. Some of the others happily joined him. They were an amusing sight, chatting together with their heads planted among the colorful wildflowers and their feet waving about slightly in the soft breezes. They had an unspoken agreement not to discuss classroom topics while taking their breaks. Their class times with Simeon were very productive and actually quite fun, but their bodies and minds needed, at least occasionally, to move away from the intensity of absorbing such new concepts.

Simeon sipped his fresh pomegranate juice and watched them from a distance. They seemed so young, so idealistic and full of zest for life. What a wonderful group of youngsters they were! Yet he knew they still had much to learn and experience.

Simeon prayed for wisdom and continuing divine guidance to lead them carefully though their first time-travel experiences. He knew that, as valuable as it was for them to learn how to time travel, there would be many pitfalls to be faced, lived through, and overcome. With these thoughts, Simeon closed his eyes and meditated. Peace flowed over him like a weightless waterfall.

After they assembled again, Thomas had more questions for Simeon. "Where exactly do other time frames exist? Are there parallel universes going on all around us, simultaneously? Is everything that has happened or ever will happen actually happening right now? Is time an illusion?"

"Perhaps standing on your head is not what you should do during break, Thomas. You're moving a little too quickly here. Please, let us take your questions slowly, one at a time.

"Where do other time frames exist? They exist in the same place that everything exists. They are a part of the Cosmic Dream stream.

"Are there parallel universes going on all around us simultaneously? Let's just say that we have as much as we can deal with in the particular universe that we seem to be experiencing right now. That's really all I can say in answer to that question for now.

"Is everything that has happened or ever will happen actually happening right now? Yes. Time, space, and life itself are an illusion — part of the 'Magic Shadow Show' which our Creator set in motion for us to both learn from and be entertained by, until we get tired of the show and merge back into oneness with God."

For the rest of their session, Simeon continued to answer questions one at a time, patiently and slowly, and as thoroughly as possible.

CHAPTER 6

Thomas had a rare free day — no classes, no teaching respon-sibilities. He decided there was time for a short trip to visit his one living family member, his younger sister Alia, who lived on another planet. Alia and Thomas were not especially close, but each was grateful to have a family member alive, and val-ued the connection. Thomas was always struck by how differ-ent in temperament and life direction he was from his sister.

Alia lived with her husband and seven children on an Earth-like planet called Blithwithi, millions of light years away from old Earth. Just before the war, when Alia was only three years old, their mother had been able to give her to a dear friend who transported her to the planet Blithwithi.

She remained on Blithwithi until she was about 30 years old. For a while, neither she nor Thomas knew that the other had survived. Finally, traveling to Earth, she found Simeon, who she'd been told was a friend of her family's.

Through Simeon she was reunited with Thomas. Thomas begged her to stay on Earth, live with him, and enter the Halls of Wisdom. But Alia had no experience with Earth and preferred her familiar life on Blithwithi. After a time, she returned and settled there permanently.

Her husband, Rebis, had come from a similar background. Though he was born on Earth, his family had fled to Blithwithi when he was still an infant, just before the Great Mantric World War III. Eventually his family returned to live on Earth, but Rebis was by that time a mature man and thoroughly used to the Blithwithian people and environment. He didn't want to live anywhere else.

Rebis and Alia met and fell in love when he was 42 and she was 40. They married and soon had children; Thomas now had four nephews and three nieces, several of whom bore a physical resemblance to him. He loved them and did his best to relate to them in a close family way.

But Alia and her family were so different from Thomas and all his Earth friends that it was difficult for them to feel close to each other.

One primary difference was that, because Blithwithia was in a lower part of its solar system's yuga cycle, Blithwithian natives were unable to speak to each other mentally. They also did not educate children in skills that Thomas took for granted — skills such as the ability to create or alter material objects, to control natural forces, to share thoughts directly with other people, or to travel through time and space with ease. Though a happy people, they seemed a bit slow and dull to Thomas.

After just a few hours with Rebis, Alia, and their children, Thomas felt exhausted from their constant, loud chatter. Alia understood, from the short time she had spent with her brother on Earth, a little of what he was experiencing with her noisy family.

Rebis was less sympathetic, never having had the slightest desire to leave Blithwithi. They quickly ran out of things to talk about; and the kids, after receiving the Earth gifts Thomas always brought with him, soon tired of their overly quiet uncle.

Thomas had told them that he couldn't stay very long this visit. Rebis, who was not an insensitive man, volunteered to take the children to the Hydrogen Looping Park so that Alia and Thomas could have some private time together.

After a little superficial chitchat and catching up, Alia decided to ask a question she'd never had the courage to ask him before. "Thomas, why have you never married or had a committed relationship with someone? I mean, ah . . . at least you've never mentioned anything like that to me." She mumbled slightly in confusion and embarrassment. Perhaps she'd overstepped his privacy needs — she was a little uncertain of the ways of the Earth-born, even though he was her brother.

Thomas looked at his little sister fondly. She was his same height and coloring. Her eyes were bright and inquisitive, but her thoughts were generally murky and closed to him. He didn't intrude mentally — that would not be courteous.

Consequently, they'd never been able to share on a deep or meaningful level.

"Dearest Alia, don't worry about my privacy issues. I don't mind your asking at all. I have never felt to look for a wife. I have had many friends of both sexes, and have some also who are not human beings, as I know you do too. But I've never found anyone who . . . well, so far there's never been anyone who's 'rung my bell.'"

They both laughed at this antique expression from old Earth times. "I have my studies with Simeon and my classes to teach. I really don't feel the need to bond with another person right now."

Even as he said these words to his sister, he knew he was not speaking the entire truth. Deep down he knew he was a bit lonely, and his sister intuitively knew it, too.

"Alia, little sister, I thank you for your concern. I think I will find someone someday, and you'll be the first to know — well, perhaps first after Simeon and a few others. I've had dreams of someone, not very clear . . . but I don't think I've met this soul yet — at least not in this lifetime. Please don't worry about me. I'm very happy, and I'm grateful that you seem happy also."

Thomas was a little puzzled by his own words, "in this lifetime." Where had that idea come from?

Alia seemed to accept what he said. She kissed his cheek. Brother and sister continued to stroll amiably around the neighborhood until it was time for them to return home, to greet her family coming back from the park.

After fond farewells, he was happy to transport himself back to his quarters on Earth to rest, meditate, and eat some fresh Earth-food. Blithwithian food was too heavy for him, though he would never tell Alia that. She fancied herself a great cook, and her family agreed with her wholeheartedly.

CHAPTER 7

After their morning meditation, Simeon began the day's class by showing them through mind pictures what they could expect to experience while time traveling.

Thomas then asked a more philosophical question. "Do we really stay in one place, while time flows by us like a river?"

Simeon replied, "You are correct in using the river as a symbol for time, for time gives us the feeling of 'flowing by.' But when you fly high above a river, you don't see its flow. You see it as a whole, from its source to its mouth. Only when you are closer to it, or 'dwelling in time,' does time seem to move."

"It is said that you can never step into the same river twice. The flowing nature of a river means it is different in every moment of time. But that difference is only relative to your place in time and space."

Simeon gave them an assignment to meditate on time as a river and to see what further clarity they could glean in superconsciousness about the nature of time. Subsequent classes were lively with discussions on the insights they'd received in meditation.

Several days later, Simeon announced that before moving forward with the topic of time travel, they needed to review the laws of karma and reincarnation. A mental sigh came from all corners of the room. They had all studied these laws at a young age, and felt sure they already understood them.

"Ah, but you don't know about karma and reincarnation in relation to time travel, do you?" Simeon smiled at their thoughts. "Stay with me on this train of thought. It's always good to review basic subjects and then look at them from slightly different or perhaps higher perspectives — yes?"

"Yes," was the consensus.

"As you know, it takes from five to eight million lifetimes of more or less automatic evolutionary stages to reach the human state — moving from 'germ to worm to human,' so to speak." The class laughed at this old joke.

"Upon achieving a human body, we also acquire a fully developed ego, which causes us to identify with our physical bodies more strongly than do animals or lower life forms. Thus we begin creating karma, which binds us to the wheel of reincarnation. One lifetime simply is not enough to work out one's desires, likes, dislikes, and so on.

"Human beings, out of ignorance, create more and more desires that must be satisfied, and thus the necessity for more lives to be lived — perhaps many millions before we come to a place of such deep dissatisfaction with what the world can give us that we are willing to turn within and seek the answer to the question of who we really are and what is the meaning of our life. Turning within marks the 'beginning of the end' of our soul's long journey through time and space, and the ultimate embracing of our oneness with God and all creation."

"Sir," said Darien, "How long does this process take?"

Simeon smiled, "It's very hard for us to imagine how long it takes — hundreds of millions of years — perhaps more."

Darien frowned, "Does it always take so long?"

"Yes, unfortunately. Desires for one thing or another take us away again and again."

Thomas once again thought, with great impatience, "We know all these teachings, Sir, but what do the laws of karma and reincarnation have to do with time travel?"

Simeon, who was the soul of patience, thought gently, "Well, what do you think, Thomas? Or any of you? It is a very important question; how would you answer it?"

Thomas should have been ready for this, for Simeon frequently gave their questions right back to them, to make them think more deeply and to evoke the answers from them, instead of simply telling them what he wanted them to learn.

Simeon continued, "Let's take this question into a brief

meditation and see what we come up with."

After a short stretching break, they had their second period of meditation that day.

Simeon began the meditation by reminding them, "Remember that the best way to receive guidance in meditation is to state the question clearly. In this case, the question is, 'What do the laws of karma and reincarnation have to do with time travel?' State the question and pray humbly for an answer, then put it aside completely and go into the inner stillness. After your time of mental stillness in superconsciousness, mentally hold the question up again, without any desires or attachment to what the answer might be or how it should be revealed to you."

The students were familiar with the process of using meditation to receive guidance in their lives. With Simeon adding his energy to theirs, the meditation seemed deeper than usual.

After an hour, Simeon chanted AUM-m-m-m-m-m-m in a deep bass voice for about five minutes. Waves of light moved up and down their spines. Thomas was reluctant to move or even to think. His one small thought was, "Who cares about the answer to this question — let me just enjoy this bliss and universal, divine Oneness a while longer."

Simeon began to sing again this old and hauntingly beautiful song:

> Through many lives I've drunk the cup of laughter:
> No man could tell the pleasures I have known.
> The stars in the endless sky,
> If one could count, would come to billions.
> Yet as vast as are their numbers,
> So many years I've wandered far from You.©

"Now, what is the answer, dear ones?" Simeon thought quietly, in order to keep the mood uplifted and calm.

Sabella surprised her fellow students by mentally and calmly answering, "Sir, in this meditation I began to see how time travel is possible. I had a vision of a great river of time with all our past lives preserved in the river's flow. When we release our attachments to the karma of this and all past lifetimes, we are able mentally to rise above the river and then re-enter it at any point we choose."

Thomas was aghast. He had "seen" the very same thing in his meditation, but had been unable to put it into words so quickly, simply, and elegantly as Sabella had just done. "I've truly underestimated her," he thought.

"Yes, you have," Simeon thought back.

Simeon nodded his approval to Sabella.

Simeon was sure now that his students understood that they would *not* be using a time machine in which to make their journeys through time. How they had laughed together at the early Dwapara Yuga concepts, illustrated books and movies of people building mechanical devices to propel them through time, as rocket ships once propelled them through space.

During their teleportation classes, they had smiled in wonderment at the idea of traveling in uncomfortable rocket ships or airplanes when it was so easy to travel using mental power.

Now, with each class, they understood more clearly, at least in theory, exactly how it would be possible to travel through time. Most of them were eager to quit talking about it and actually try it. Simeon seemed constantly to be slowing them down when they wanted to get on with it!

Finally, sensing their mounting impatience, Simeon called a halt to their discussions and gave them some exciting news. "Let us close for today. When we resume class day after tomorrow, we will try a time-travel session with one or more of you, to see how you react to an actual trip to another time and place. For this evening and until we meet again, meditate and pray for help and guidance. I will do so also.

"Remember: time travel is not to be taken lightly or to be seen as a pleasure jaunt. What happens to you may have a strong psychological impact on you, for you will be experiencing how you lived and what you felt in an earlier lifetime. Be sure you feel ready to do this. There is no harm in waiting, or shame in deciding you don't care to participate right away.

"You can wait to observe its effect on others who go before you, or you can opt out altogether. Time travel is not for everyone. I have observed each of you carefully for many years and feel you are ready. Still, I want to be very sure that *you* feel you have the courage, willpower, and mental strength to time-travel well. Go within yourselves now and be absolutely certain about this major step in your life. God bless and keep you!"

CHAPTER 8

The morning dawned cool and clear, as all mornings tended to do during this part of Treta Yuga. Weather control had become an almost perfected science.

Thomas was excited. He tried to dampen his enthusiasm at least a little. He knew Simeon encouraged enthusiasm in his students, but he also wanted them to remain centered and calm under all circumstances — no small order, indeed!

Arriving at the class site early, he was surprised to see most of his classmates there before him; they must be sharing his anticipation. Thomas smiled at Sabella, who looked especially subdued.

"Are you ready to begin?" he queried her.

"Yes, how about you?"

"Yes, I feel ready, willing, and able — I really want to be first or in the first group — but of course we need to see who Simeon feels should be our class's first 'traveler.' If you are chosen, I wish you many blessings."

"And you also," she smiled at him with her expressive eyes.

Simeon, unusually, was a little late to class. Always he was there to greet them, no matter how early they arrived. He offered no explanation for his lateness, but simply began speaking to them mentally in his dynamic way.

"I know that most of you have anticipated this day for a long time. I have observed each of you and tried to evaluate your readiness for this venture. Vilma and Luwitin have asked to wait and see the effects on those who travel before them. This is perfectly fine — and even wise of them, for you are undertaking an activity with which you have no personal experience. As I have said many times, it may have a surprising effect on you.

"After much deliberation and meditation, I have chosen Sabella, Darien, and Thomas to be our first time travelers." He smiled brightly at the three students, who were doing their best to remain calm.

Those not chosen also did their best not to be disappointed; they knew their chance would come soon. One or two realized they were secretly glad to observe first and travel later!

"Because of your present lack of experience with actual time travel, I have chosen the time and place to which each of you will travel today. Later, you will have more choice about where and when you choose to go.

"You will each stay four months standard Earth-time, while only four days will pass here, during the time you are 'away.' Since this is mental travel, I and the other class members will watch over your bodies while you are away. In four days, you will return to body awareness, unless for any reason I feel it necessary to help you return sooner. Remember that I will be 'with' you, although not in observation of *every* moment, but always conscious of your whereabouts and well-being. You will not feel my presence, for you will only know yourself as that body and personality you once were.

"You will enter your past life fully and re-live it during the time you are there, just as you lived it when it happened. You will retain a full memory of that life, from its beginning to the point in time when you return here. After you return to this body, time, and place, you will rest, eat, sleep, and meditate for as long as I feel you need it — usually this 're-entry' time takes two or three days.

"Then we'll begin the process of debriefing, finding out what you learned about yourself and the yuga in which you were living. The first part of the debriefing will be one-on-one with me. Then, if you are willing, you may share your experiences with the rest of our class. We'll discuss the impact of re-living a segment of your past, and what you learned from it.

"Is this all clear? Now is the time for final questions from any of you."

Silence prevailed.

CHAPTER 9

Thomas became aware of sitting beside a river. For a moment he felt a combination of disorientation and *déjà vu.*

He turned to the woman sitting beside him and said, "Dearest, what yuga is this?"

She laughed at the old joke and answered as she always did. "It's 1,808 years until the end of Descending Treta Yuga. Want to be somewhere else? I'm sure it can be arranged."

With this she shed her clothes and plunged into the river. He followed her quickly and splashed her good-naturedly. Then they began a three-mile swim up the sparkling river, pulling against a medium-strong current. It was a good workout, one they enjoyed frequently.

The downstream part was easier, of course. From time to time they simply floated and let the current carry them along, while they listened to the river's quiet music. Upon returning to their point of origin, they sprawled on a sandbar and let the sun warm and soothe their tired muscles.

Sunitia soon drifted off to sleep. Thomas felt drowsy also, but resisted sleep to enjoy looking at his wife — the love of his life — as she slept peacefully in the sunshine. A little smile was on her lips — perhaps in response to one of her unusual dreams, dreams she loved to share with Thomas.

Often when he looked at Sunitia, Thomas wondered at his great good fortune in being married to this lovely woman. He offered a prayer of thanksgiving for having known her when they were both children, for being her dearest friend through most of this lifetime, and for the deep bond between them, a bond which eventually led to their lifetime commitment to each other in marriage.

A memory came to him of many children playing in the river years ago — actually not far from where they were resting now. Mothers or older siblings were watching the little ones, but not carefully enough. Sunitia, in her usual boldness, had moved beyond the safe area of the river and had become caught in its strong current. She was probably only four years old at the time; Thomas would have been about six. He saw what she was doing and yelled to her to be careful, but it was too late. Panic-stricken to see her being swept away, he immediately plunged into the strong current and swam after her as best he could.

Fortunately, his fifteen-year-old brother and her eighteen-year-old sister heard his yell and took action immediately, calling to the adults for help. Both children were saved from drowning, but Thomas now remembered vividly those moments of racing after Sunitia's small, receding form in the river and praying that she would not be taken away from him forever.

During those fleeting moments trying to reach her, he had a strange experience. He felt himself lifted out of his body, high above the river, where he could see their small bodies moving along swiftly — Sunitia flailing about in panic, and Thomas a few feet behind her, swimming valiantly to reach her.

In that moment he felt at peace, though he knew they were both in great danger. But the most striking thing about his experience was that he saw a golden aura of light surrounding each of them, and a golden cord of light connecting them. He felt overwhelmingly loved and blessed in that moment and absolutely assured that not only would they be saved from drowning, but that their lives were forever linked in a mysterious and perfect way.

And then he was back in the swift river and had reached her, grabbing and holding onto her with all his six-year-old strength, holding her head above the water until their older siblings were able to reach them and pull them to safety.

Sunitia claimed to remember very little about this event — after all, she was only four. But the experience was indelibly engraved in Thomas's memory as one of the most important moments of his life. Indeed, from that day forward he took his swimming lessons with much greater seriousness and insisted that she do so also.

From that moment forward they were both slightly aware of their deep bond, though they seldom thought about it. They were friends and schoolmates, but both had many other friends and often had very different interests. It took some time for the depth of their connection to become real to them.

When Thomas was about twenty-five years old, he went to school on another planet for ten years and thus was separated from Sunitia, his family, and other friends. Although he came home for visits, it was a difficult time for him, because by now he was aware of his growing love for Sunitia. He felt she loved him in return, though they had not yet spoken of it.

Upon his final return home with a double degree in xenobiology and ancient history, they were happily reunited and were able to express their love for each other. They began making plans to be married. Both sets of parents approved the choice, but urged them to wait. It was unusual to life-link at that young age and it was felt that Sunitia, especially, needed more time to study, travel, and become her own person. Bowing to parental pressure, they agreed to wait while Sunitia completed her schooling and traveled off-planet for a time.

But physical separation became increasingly painful for both of them. They finally decided that no matter what their family and friends thought about their decision and whatever life might hold for them, they must be together. They found their thoughts increasingly linked, as though they were one being — even if their bodies were light years apart. Their minds were usually in perfect harmony. They rarely spoke to each other aloud — only if they were with others who were unable to use "mind-speak" as easily as they were.

In this part of Descending Treta Yuga, many mental skills were becoming less common. Children were being born now who seemed virtually un-trainable in the mental and psychic abilities that had been common only a generation or two earlier.

Thomas and Sunitia were ceremonially life-linked ten years ago. They settled in a villa near their birthplace and began the occupations they loved and had trained for. Thomas was a historian in the local Learning Halls. Sunitia was an architect/designer and taught architectural skills to older children. She was also a brilliant dream-researcher/guide, loved and revered by her colleagues even at her young age.

Now, as they lazed on the sunny sands, Thomas gazed at her peaceful face and her closed eyes moving a little in sleep — she was probably in the middle of an interesting dream. Filled with gratitude for his life with her, Thomas thought how incomplete he would feel without her. "Do all lovers feel this way?" he wondered.

Sunitia was somewhat shorter than many women in this age, about 6 feet 8 inches. Her athletic swimmer's body was lean, somewhat muscular, and beautiful to behold. Her long, black hair, now wet from her swim, was spread around her head in lovely disarray. Her eyes were dark brown — amazing in their depth and sparkle. Her skin was olive-tone, easily darkened by the sunshine.

Sunitia stirred and opened her eyes to see Thomas frowning at her. "Why the frown, beloved?"

"Just lost in rambling thoughts of not too much importance." He smiled and changed the subject. "What were you dreaming?"

Now it was her turn to knit her brow in concentration. "Ah, yes, it was a dream which comes to me often these days. I was designing a structure — I think it was a temple. It was made of energy or light rays or something like that — in the shape of a pyramid. I felt an urgency to design it well and quickly. I sensed that the knowledge of how to manifest such a building was slipping away from me faster than I could get the project done. In my dream, people kept interrupting me, saying, 'Why are you going so slowly? Why haven't you finished it! Time is slipping away. Time is of the essence!'"

Thomas was surprised to see tears in her eyes as she transmitted her dream pictures to his mind. He found he also was disturbed by her dream. He'd had similar thoughts recently of the unusual urgency to complete his present project in the Learning Halls.

He had been working to create a body of learning materials called "Time-Traveling Techniques in Treta Yuga." The project had recently reached an impasse for reasons that were puzzling to Thomas, and somewhat similar to what Sunitia described.

Thomas took her in his arms and opened his heart and mind to her, for their mutual comfort. "Sunitia, we both know that in a descending yuga such as we are in now, knowledge does slip away. Those who come after will not be able to access the same knowledge that we take for granted as common and easy to comprehend. This change should not be sad for us or disturb our work — rather it should motivate us to preserve what we can, so that our children, grandchildren, and future generations will be able to access and use the stored knowledge of what has come before them."

Sunitia relaxed in his arms and sighed. "Yes, I know all that you say is true, but when these dreams come to me — and they do so often lately — I feel I'm not doing enough to preserve this knowledge. Information is being lost more quickly than it can be preserved. Ways of preserving it are falling apart."

"Today, here, now! That is the important thing for us. The Great Spirit and our wise elders will guide us in how best to carry out our work to help future generations."

She turned to look into the sweet blue-green eyes of her first and only love. "Well, you mentioned our grandchildren. How do you propose we'll manage that if we have no children?"

Her sparkling laughter lit up the beautiful afternoon, as Thomas sat back and looked at her with great surprise. They had thought about having children, of course, but never seriously, as they were still young and immersed in their work and in each other. It was mutually understood that starting a family was years in the future.

"Are you not-so-subtly hinting at something, my dear?"

"Well-l-l-l, maybe so. What do you think about our having a child sooner rather than later?"

"Sunitia, we life-linked earlier than is recommended. What would everyone say if we jumped ahead on this one also?"

She smiled charmingly. "Since when have we ever acted as others do? And besides, things are changing around us in so many ways. Perhaps there is a message to us in what we see and feel in these changes. You and I feel adamant about preserving worthwhile knowledge for future generations. Perhaps teaching our own children would be one more way of doing this — perhaps the best way of all!"

"Dearest, I may still need further convincing. Let's meditate and pray for guidance."

The lengthening afternoon shadows found the couple sitting together, side by side, their backs straight and tall, their eyes closed, and their faces radiant in inner communion.

CHAPTER 10

Thomas sat in the local Learning Hall with his young apprentice, Timron.

Three months had passed since that sunny afternoon by the river. Sunitia was two months pregnant with their first child. They had decided to try a less conventional type of conception and gestation procedure. She was actually carrying the child in her womb. Why they had chosen to do this was still a mystery to them, but still it seemed right to them.

When Thomas thought of his unborn daughter (Sunitia had insisted on a daughter and he was fine with the decision), he was filled with great joy. So far, they had shielded their minds from everyone about what they had done — knowing it would cause a great uproar among friends and family.

"Timron!" Thomas called out loudly to his assistant. Timron was watching a local flash-report on his mind-screen — hoping Thomas wouldn't notice. Thomas always noticed, but often didn't bother to disturb Timron. This time, however, he knew that a simple mind-tap wouldn't work and verbally called his name.

Timron started violently and stuttered, "Er-r-r yes, sir? I mean, did you think me something and I didn't hear it, or. . . ."

"Never mind, Timron. Let's get started on today's project. Were you able to complete the research I asked you to do a few days ago?"

"Yes — well, 'complete' is probably not the right word, but I got a start on it."

"Let me know what you learned."

Timron said enthusiastically, "Well, I interviewed Archival Elder Longtraveler as you instructed."

"Please, Timron," Thomas interrupted. "Don't give your

report by speaking out loud. I want your report to be given to me mentally, with word-pictures accompanying it — just as I've instructed you."

Timron hung his head and blushed. "Sorry, sir," he thought as calmly as possible. "It's just so much more difficult to do that than to speak out loud. I feel I'm going to burst a blood vessel in my head when I communicate mentally. I understand why you want me to do it, but it's very hard — and hardly anyone does it anymore, except for a few old-timers!"

Realizing what he had just implied, Timron blushed even more deeply. He knew that Thomas wasn't that much older than he.

Thomas laughed. "I know it's difficult, perhaps even quaint these days, but it's needed for the important project I've asked you to help me with. Spoken words never convey the truth as clearly as mental communication. I can accept nothing else from you at this time. So, please proceed. If you become too tired from the effort, let me know and we'll rest and do something else."

Timron bravely launched into mental communication. Once he relaxed and got further into the process, he found it wasn't that hard to communicate mentally. It was a flow, and indeed it was much more efficient.

Timron revealed that, though at first he was intimidated by so noble a personage as Elder Longtraveler, she had turned out to be a very kind and gracious woman. He had thoroughly enjoyed being with her and obtaining the information Thomas had requested.

Time-travel techniques were known by only a handful of people these days — Thomas being one of the few who had expressed interest in learning how to do it. Not many people alive had actually time traveled or even wanted to hear more about it. Most people wondered why anyone would want to try something so risky. The prevailing rumors were that time travel could not be mentally or physically healthy. Other rumors reported (falsely) that people had "left" never to return to the present time. Thomas was hoping to dispel these false ideas among the general population.

And even more important, he wanted to see if he could try time travel himself. He had not told this last part to Sunitia, especially now that she was carrying their first child. He knew it might be upsetting to her. She seemed so much more sensitive now, and that was saying something, because she had always seemed the most open and empathic person he'd ever met. But he knew that pregnancy changed a woman in many ways.

Sunitia was becoming more and more dear to Thomas, if that were possible, as she lovingly carried their first daughter. They were both having fun communicating with this little soul, as she grew in Sunitia's womb. Even at this early stage, she seemed to have a willful personality.

"Uh, sir, do you want me to go on with my report?" thought Timron.

"Caught me mentally wandering, did you? Sorry about that! Please continue."

"Congratulations on your wife's pregnancy." Timron beamed.

"Oops, you really were eavesdropping on my thoughts, weren't you?"

"I thought we were supposed to be communicating mentally." Timron was jokingly sarcastic with his boss — something he rarely dared to do.

"Thank you for your congratulations! Please keep our good news to yourself. Now proceed!"

Timron's assignment had been to interview Elder Longtraveler about her experiences with time travel. Rumor was that she had done it many times in years past. If this rumor was true, Thomas wanted to know what techniques she had used and what she had learned from her experiences.

At first Elder had spoken sparingly and quietly to her young interviewer. Though polite, she seemed reluctant to give him many details. She shyly mentioned that she had traveled backward through time on fifteen occasions, and in the process she had learned much about several past ages.

As she spoke Timron had felt her watching him carefully, for the slightest sign of skepticism on his part. It was obvious that she had been disbelieved or even ridiculed for revealing what had happened to her while time traveling.

Having caught the "time-travel fever" from Thomas many months previously, Timron had no skepticism to show; he was *intensely* interested in what Elder Longtraveler had to say. Elder sensed his sincere interest and began to open up more and more to her new young friend, sharing stories that were exciting, unusual, and sometimes almost unbelievable. Still, Timron believed her — her words rang with truth.

Making his report to Thomas, he bubbled with enthusiasm to share what Elder Longtraveler had told him.

Thomas listened with amusement to his enthusiastic apprentice. Timron's red hair seemed to stand up on his head when he became excited, which he did often. Red hair was rarely seen these days; it had become very scarce in the gene pool. Thomas liked it. Timron didn't; he had been teased too often about his unusual "carrot top."

Though enjoying Elder Longtraveler's stories, Thomas interrupted Timron and asked, "Excuse me. Her stories are very interesting, but did you get the chance to ask her if she would share her techniques for time travel with me?"

"Yes, and she told me to send you to her whenever you wanted to visit. She seemed very open to sharing with you — or with anyone interested in the subject. Her last words to me were, 'Come back again, dear boy. So few are interested in this subject. You were a wonderful listener.'"

"Ah, just as I suspected. She is growing old and sees that important knowledge is being lost or forgotten with each passing year. Thank you, Timron. I will visit her as soon as possible."

Timron couldn't resist. "When she teaches you to travel through time, will you teach me also? I want to go with you!"

"We shall see, Timron, after I understand more thoroughly what is involved. But I'm very glad to find someone like you who is sincerely interested in the subject. As you know, people seem either ignorant or fearful of time travel these days."

CHAPTER 11

Returning home that evening, Thomas was surprised to see Sunitia waiting for him on the porch, dressed to go out for the evening.

"Sunitia, what's going on? Did I forget something we're supposed to do this evening?"

"No, dearest. But there is somewhere I want you to go with me — something I want you to see. But first, please tell me what happened today."

Thomas sat beside her to tell what he'd heard about Elder Longtraveler and what he hoped to learn from her about time traveling.

Sunitia frowned slightly at the thought of Thomas leaving her and traveling through time, but wouldn't allow herself to say or even think a negative word about it, for she knew how important it was for him to investigate the subject personally and thoroughly.

When he had finished sharing his news, he asked curiously, "So where are we going?"

"Close your eyes, hold my hand, and I'll take you there," she said. It was not like her to hide things from him, but he could see she was taking delight in this surprise. Many years ago they had learned to travel through space together, "in tandem" so to speak, one carrying the other along to his or her destination of choice.

"Open your eyes now," she thought to him excitedly.

Thomas was not sure where they were, or even if they were still on planet Earth. He was astonished to see before him a huge, golden pyramid. Sunitia was transmitting a thought to him now that this building was very similar to the one she'd seen in her recent dream. "Remember when we were resting by the river and I told you about my dream of the great golden pyramid made of light?"

They were standing on a high hill overlooking a lush green valley with a large river flowing through it. The golden pyramid stood huge and silent on the banks of the river. As Thomas looked more carefully, he could see that there were other pyramids in the distance, also along the river, stretching as far as they could see.

"Thomas, there are seven of them!" she thought, reading his wonderment at what they were actually seeing. "They represent the chakras, the centers of energy along our own inner river, our astral spine."

"They are magnificent! Where are we? What is this place?"

"We are on Earth," Sunitia revealed. "We are in a secret river valley, unknown to almost everyone on this planet."

"How did you find out about it?"

"This place was revealed to me in a dream, only today, when I was napping this afternoon. I was told where it is and how to get here. I came and saw what we are seeing now, plus a bit more. Then I decided to wait until you returned home to share this with you. I want to be sure I'm not still dreaming." She beamed her bewitching smile at him.

"You're not," he thought to her, "unless we are both dreaming the same dream. What shall we do now?"

"Let's explore — I think we are expected!" She grasped his hand and teleported them to the edge of the river, near the closest golden pyramid.

Very close to the first pyramid now, they were both in awe at its size, but more than that, at the magnetic radiance and energy it was emitting. It seemed to be made of sunbeams or some other sort of vibrating light.

"What now?" they both thought together.

Just at that moment, they noticed a robed figure sitting nearby. They were reasonably sure he had just materialized there. He made no movement and seemed to be meditating.

They looked at each other, sharing a knowing glance. They

walked quietly to where he sat, and sat on either side of him, assuming their own meditative poses. Intuitively they knew that he would speak to them only when he was ready to do so. Perhaps he needed to "read" their thoughts or feel their energy patterns. His vibrations were benevolent and extremely powerful.

Soon they were lost in the silence, calm and uplifted. After a time, the man began to sing a song in a language unknown to them — it was glorious and soothing, a lovely way to end a meditation. At its close, he opened his eyes and smiled at them.

"Sunitia, thank you for coming and for bringing Thomas along. You are a receptive dreamer, and thus I am happy to be able to show you this place now."

Sunitia smiled at this stranger who seemed to know her and Thomas, and said, "We are honored to be here, sir. Who are you? Where are we exactly and what is going on?"

"I am Brother Solonar, an architect like you, Sunitia."

"Well, thank you, sir. You do me honor, calling *me* an architect in the presence of these . . . pyramids? Are you the creator of these — whatever they are?" Sunitia asked in eager awe.

"Co-creator with the Divine Presence and many others also, both physical and astral beings," Solonar said quietly. "You are blessed to be able to see them. They are known to few on Earth. They were created as a reminder of certain important inner realities, the knowledge of which is being lost as this present age descends into a lower one. They will exist much longer than the memory of how they were made or why. The sands of time will blow over them, figuratively and literally, before their message is once again revealed to those who crave the knowledge they can reveal."

"May we see them? I mean, may we enter them — at least one of them? Can you tell me how they were made, architecturally speaking?" Sunitia was glowing in her enthusiasm. "They are so magnificent, so beautiful, and so perfect in symmetry and form. How long have they been here?"

"Be calm, my little sister. I will be your guide and tell you what you want to know. You will enjoy your tour, I know."

With these thought-words, Solonar stood up and led them toward the first golden pyramid of light.

CHAPTER 12

It was difficult to know how long they'd been gone that evening. Now Thomas lay awake in their bed, holding his exhausted and soundly sleeping wife in his arms. As she slept, he reviewed all they had seen and learned from the mysterious Brother Solonar.

Thomas had understood far less about the architecture than Sunitia, but he knew that what they had seen was beyond any construction either of them had imagined possible. The location of the "Valley of the Golden Pyramids," as they began to call it, had been secretly revealed to them. They were courteously but firmly asked to keep the location to themselves, a request to which they readily agreed.

The metaphysical construction methods were also to remain secret, including the "why" behind their creation. Thomas would leave it to Sunitia, with her architecturally trained mind, to understand exactly *how* the pyramids had been constructed.

He felt more drawn to understand the *why's* of the pyramids' existence. Solonar had revealed that among their various functions, the seven golden pyramids were to serve in the future as historical memory banks — or "wisdom preservers," as he called them.

History and how it affects and defines the future were among Thomas's specialties. He realized that there was much still to be understood. So much was being lost in this age. So much knowledge to try to preserve — somehow! He was grateful to meet Solonar and learn that he was not alone in his desire to serve the world in this way.

Solonar told them that the pyramids were also places of spiritual initiation, and strongly hinted to Thomas and Sunitia that they might, in future, want to consider taking the initiation in the pyramids. Both felt drawn to pursue this path.

As dawn approached and the birds began singing, Thomas smiled at his sleeping wife and loved her more deeply than ever before. What a joy to share this life with his beloved. No matter what the future might bring, they were joined together in their hearts, linked forever in every way: soul mates, if ever such existed. In many ways, he was certain of little in this rapidly changing age — but one thing he knew without question: the deep and loving connection between them was a connection of souls, a connection both timeless and endless.

Several days later, Thomas was granted his long-desired interview with Elder Longtraveler. They talked of time travel and of many related things. She smiled when he mentally "let slip" a hint about the Valley of the Golden Pyramids; their image was so strong in his conscious thoughts — that it was difficult to shield them from her.

He realized what he had done and was about to beg her to forget these thoughts. She surprised him by saying, "Thomas, I know Brother Solonar well. We communicate frequently. It was I who told him that you and your lovely wife would be excellent people with whom to share this precious knowledge. Your secret is my secret."

Thomas was thrilled with this news. They talked so late into the night about the wonders of the Golden Pyramids that Thomas almost forgot his initial mission, to ask her to reveal time-travel techniques to him. But he could see she was growing tired — she was, after all, well over 200 years old.

Elder Longtraveler twinkled at him with her sparkling, violet eyes and said, "Yes, although I sleep very little these days, some rest is needed now. Come tomorrow and I will teach you what you want to know."

With this clear reassurance ringing in his mind, Thomas went home to share his news with Sunitia.

CHAPTER 13

Sunitia was happy for Thomas, for she knew how much the secrets of time travel meant to him, and quite possibly to the whole civilization. But knowing of his deep desire to time travel did not stop her from worrying about his safety. After all, they had a daughter on the way!

Her heart told her constantly that she needed his *physical* presence with her during these months. He assured her that when he time-traveled, he would not be away from her very long — somewhere between a day and a week. He also told her that Elder Longtraveler would guide him and there would be no danger to him in any way. Still she fretted a bit, and all the while did her best to hide her fears from him. She reminded herself that no matter what happened they were linked soul to soul.

"Today's the day!" Thomas awoke Sunitia with a happy morning kiss. "Elder will show me the techniques of time travel and perhaps even let me try a short trip."

"Where will you go, beloved? Will you be very far back in time?"

"I feel it's best to let Elder Longtraveler decide what is best for my first venture."

"You'll let me know before you go and how long you'll be away?" Sunitia couldn't fully hide her fears.

"Of course! Please don't be concerned. I'll be back before you know I'm gone." Thomas's face was full of smiles as he dressed, ate a small breakfast, and left their home.

Sunitia knew very well what she needed. She went to their lovely little meditation temple, overlooking the river just behind their home. Interestingly enough, she had designed it as a small pyramid — many years before knowing anything about the Valley of the Golden Pyramids. The pyramid shape had attracted Sunitia all her life. She was known for incorporating it into almost all of her architectural designs.

Just a few minutes into the silence and stillness were enough to bring her to a point of peace and clarity. She knew that Thomas, the baby in her womb, and she herself — all were encompassed by God's light and love. Time and distance were meaningless in this place of inner peace. After a few hours of meditation, she arose to meet the day with a smile of contentment, free from all fears. She sent Thomas a strong mental blessing and words of love and confidence.

When he received the inner message from Sunitia, Thomas was sitting, listening to Elder Longtraveler explain how she could assist him in a visit to the past. Elder caught the thought, too, even though it had not been directed to her, for it was very strong. She smiled and said: "Do you want to take a moment to reply to Sunitia?"

"Thank you," Thomas said, and did so. Sunitia told him she had heard from Brother Solonar again and received an invitation for another visit to the Pyramids. She was happy and excited about the invitation and wanted to find out when Thomas was free to accompany her there again.

After a break for lunch at noon, Elder Longtraveler spoke another hour or so and finally asked Thomas if he felt prepared to undertake a small journey in time. He asked her several questions to clarify all that she had transferred into his mind. Then he spoke slowly and carefully: "Yes, I am ready to go now. Will you tell me when and where I'll be going?"

"Certainly! I thought it best not to go too far back for this first time out and to not stay very long. You'll spend about twelve hours in a lifetime you lived 300 years ago. You'll feel as though a day is passing for you there. A single day won't give you much time to acclimate, but since you'll be experiencing a time not so long ago, relatively speaking, you should adjust quickly to being there. I'll be monitoring you all the way, so there's nothing to fear."

She continued, "Let's pray and meditate for an hour now, and then you'll be on your way."

After an hour, she brought them both gently out of meditation chanting AUM-m-m-m softly, and then mentally asked, "Are you ready, Thomas?"

His shining eyes gave her the answer.

As excited as he was about his first time-travel experience, Thomas remembered to contact Sunitia to let her know when and where he was going and for how long.

It was very late when he returned home that night. He was surprised to find her sleeping peacefully. He had feared she might worry or not be able to sleep. "That shows you don't know everything!" she softly thought, not coming fully awake. "Your daughter and I need our rest. Tell me all about it in the morning."

Gratefully, he left her sleeping and went to his office to write down his exciting experiences while they were still clear in his mind.

In the morning, he shared the details with Sunitia, and later with his young assistant, Timron, who had been waiting (somewhat impatiently) to hear about his first time-travel adventure.

The following weeks passed rapidly, with Thomas absorbing more and more from Elder Longtraveler, and, with her permission, passing it along, first to Timron and then to a few other interested students.

He carefully chronicled his discoveries. His time away changed from hours to days, until finally Elder Longtraveler declared him ready to proceed alone, if he wished to try it. He had a destination and time picked out, many thousands of years in the past. He had told Sunitia that he'd be away for a week and asked if she was content with this idea.

"Perhaps 'contentment' is not the right word. 'Acceptance' is a better one. And I'm pleased to see you so happy with this new aspect of your work. I *do* trust now that you'll be back to share with me and with others what you've learned. I will miss your physical presence of course, but I know our connection is always there. My love and prayers go with you."

Thus, with his new knowledge and experience and with his wife's and Elder Longtraveler's blessings, he launched himself joyfully into a long-ago and far-away place.

CHAPTER 14

"Thomas!" Simeon was mentally, but very forcefully calling his name. "Thomas! Be present. Be here in this time and place. The journey into your past is over now."

Thomas slowly opened his eyes to look into Simeon's calm silver eyes. He knew who Simeon was. He knew who he was — the same Thomas he had always been. He knew where he was, in the Halls of Wisdom. He knew the year was 5910 AD, (1,810 years into Ascending Treta Yuga). Beyond that, he was amazingly unsteady and unsure about what was real and what was not.

Seeing his disorientation, Simeon was somewhat concerned. Most time travelers, even "first timers," returned with little or no feeling of being dazed or confused. He had soothing "wake-up" tea and some crackers and spread brought for Thomas to drink and eat.

"Don't talk for a little while — wait until you feel more solid and present in this time frame." Simeon was loving but firm with him.

"Sir?" he finally spoke aloud. "Sir?" His voice cracked and was very soft — he was not used to speaking aloud.

"Quietly, Thomas. We have plenty of time to exchange thoughts about what you experienced."

"Sir! Forgive me for speaking out loud, but I'm afraid that's all I can manage at the moment and I feel I must communicate with you right now! I know where I am. I know what has happened to me and where and when I've been, but. . . ." And here Thomas broke into loud sobs.

Simeon was now very concerned. Surely he had not so badly miscalculated the readiness of this brilliant young man for his first time-travel experience. It was difficult for him to believe that his preparation of Thomas had been incomplete in some way.

"Peace, my son! Whatever is wrong, we'll face it together. I know about the lifetime, the yuga, and the place you visited. It was not a violent time. What could possibly have happened to affect you this way?"

"Sunitia! My life, my love. Where is she? Is she lost to me forever?" His sobs continued undiminished.

"Ah-h-h, I understand. Sunitia was your wife in that time." Simeon respectfully retreated into inner silence.

After a little while, Thomas was able to control his emotions. But he turned away from his teacher, shoulders slumping, head lowered.

"Sir, I need some time to be alone."

"No, you don't!" Simeon's thought transference sprang at him as forcefully as Thomas remembered ever experiencing.

Unable to stand the bright light of Simeon's face, Thomas stood and raced from his teacher's presence, a picture of misery and confusion. But even in this state, he was able to send a final thought to Simeon. "Sir, forgive me. I'll be back tomorrow. Please, I must go — somewhere. I must think this through."

Simeon said or thought nothing more. He simply sat down and began to meditate and pray deeply for Thomas.

Hours later, Thomas found himself at his special spot by the shining river. He was lying face down, gripping the sweet grass that grew beneath him, trying to calm himself and think clearly.

After a time he felt somewhat calmer, and he was able to put a few thoughts together in a coherent way: "I wanted so badly to travel back through time. I wanted to see the past, to learn from it . . . and I *did* learn — ah, so many things about that long-ago life and that segment of a Descending Treta Yuga, so much like this time I am living in now and yet so different in many ways.

"In this Ascending Treta Yuga, we are obviously moving into greater and greater knowledge, and there, in Descending

Treta Yuga, knowledge was steadily being lost. It was bitter-sweet to know this and yet I felt impelled to hang on to whatever knowledge I could — the urgency I felt to leave a legacy to those coming after us. . . ." Here he paused and burst into tears again, for he felt the newly-awakened memories of that long-ago lifetime coming quickly to him now. What about his unborn daughter? And of course, with that vibrant memory, he began to drown in memories of his wife, his beautiful Sunitia. Sweet memories of his lifetime with her, so long, long ago, flooded in all at once and began to overwhelm him.

Thomas felt as though he had been torn into two pieces, and one of those pieces was completely lost in the river of time.

"Sunitia!" he sent out this thought as strongly as he could, to touch her, to find her! "Sunitia, can you hear me? I'm here, where are you?"

He called and called for a long time.

No answer came. All he could hear were the gurgling sounds of the river flowing by.

Exhausted by this uncharacteristic emotional turmoil, he finally went home to bed and prayed for respite in sleep. Surprisingly, sleep came; in the morning, he awoke feeling slightly clearer and more grounded in himself. He meditated for a time, went for a swim, then calmly prepared himself to see Simeon, who he knew would be patiently waiting for him in the Halls of Wisdom.

By now Thomas had a plan of sorts. He would simply explain to Simeon that he needed to go back to Sunitia and live in *that* lifetime, in Descending Treta Yuga, and not stay here in this time frame. That was the only solution — of this he was now sure. It was impossible for him to live without her.

CHAPTER 15

Simeon was alone, meditating, waiting for Thomas. Thomas sat near him and began to meditate too.

After a time, Simeon sent a quiet thought to Thomas: "I've given your classmates the day off. I wanted time and privacy to talk with you and to help you through this test you are facing. That was quite an emotional outburst from you yesterday! Are you feeling better today?"

Thomas knew that his intuitive teacher was just being polite. Simeon well knew his state of mind. He knew everything about him! Usually Thomas was grateful for his teacher's knowledge of his inner turmoil, but this morning he felt irritated and quarrelsome.

"Sir, you know what is going on with me. What more do I need to reveal to you? I want your permission and blessing to return to Sunitia, my wife, and continue my life there with her. I feel more than half dead without her by my side, and I must be with her. Life is simply not worth living without her."

Silence from Simeon.

Thomas continued, "I *know* what you are thinking. You warned us about this sort of danger in our preparatory classes on time travel. You explained that we'd be only 'dipping' into a past time by re-living a small section of one of our past lives, but that we could not do more than that. It is not wise for a new time traveler, you said, to leave this present life for more than a short time. I remember all this. But Sir, I didn't know . . . I just didn't understand how much I could love someone." Here, he broke down again in tears.

"How could I have known this? How could anyone be prepared to find a lost love like my beloved Sunitia, and then let her go without a backward glance? Sir, I must return to her soon. Life has no other meaning for me now. Please help me!"

Simeon was a compassionate man. His heart was attuned to

the broken heart of his dear student, so much so that he could feel the pain, the grief, and more than that, Thomas's great confusion. He thought about the hundreds of young people he had assisted in time-travel experiences. He had seen this sort of thing happen before, but *never* had he known a pupil who had been so profoundly affected by meeting a loved one from the past. Usually after a few days, some meditation and talking it through, the past attachment receded into memory, the needed lessons were learned, and life went on.

He was reasonably sure that time would heal Thomas's grief. Thomas needed time to become re-involved with other people and projects here, in this time frame, and to feel ready to go on with his life. He was not sure that Thomas would agree with this solution, but he had to try.

"Thomas," he thought softly but firmly, "we shall not rule out your returning to be with Sunitia at some point. But for now, you must stay here in this time and go on with your lifetime in the here and now. I want you to continue your studies with me, but in a slightly different way. Your primary project for the next month will be to chronicle the time-travel journey from which you have just returned.

"Because of the dramatic impact your visit has had on you, I want you to spend more time on this than would be usual, in silence and seclusion, processing what you've learned, getting it into a record from which you and others might learn. It is best that you not speak with your fellow students about what has happened to you. You'll meet with me alone, once every other day, so that we can review your project. At the end of the month. . . ." Simeon paused in his thoughts.

"Then I can return to her?" Thomas said.

Simeon directed his thoughts to Thomas: "We shall see."

"Tell it to me straight," Thomas demanded. "Is this just your way of putting me off? Are you hoping that time will help me see the error of my ways? If so, I can tell you now that it won't work! I must return to her!"

Simeon was amazed at the strength of Thomas's desire, and

the powerful energy he was blasting out in all directions. But he simply said, "Thomas, will you do as I ask? Have I ever guided you wrongly in the past?"

Thomas slowly became calmer. He began to recall the years and years of unconditional love and endless patience that Simeon had given him, never asking for anything in return.

"I will do as you ask," Thomas said and knelt at Simeon's feet for a blessing. Simeon gave it willingly, thanking the Divine for the intervention in this potentially dangerous situation. Teacher and student went their separate ways.

CHAPTER 16

Thomas was surprised at how quickly the time passed for him during the next four weeks. It was soothing to meditate much more than usual, to let go of his other duties and be almost completely alone. He met with Simeon briefly once every other day, as his teacher had requested.

Surprisingly, Simeon came to his home for these meetings, something he had done only rarely in the past. Their meetings were very quiet and rarely lasted more than thirty minutes. Thomas never spoke aloud, nor did Simeon. Their thought transferences were calm, with Simeon asking a few questions and receiving the new section of the chronicle Thomas had just finished, at the close of each visit.

Simeon never corrected or lectured Thomas during these quiet weeks. He simply poured out love and blessings to him.

Thomas found some solace in reliving the memories of the months he had spent with Sunitia. His dreams at night were only of her. His thoughts revolved around her during the day as he sought to remember and chronicle every moment of their time together, describing in minute detail where they had lived, what they had done together, what he had learned from it, how that age was different from this one and how it was alike. He especially loved remembering the shining golden pyramids in the beautiful river valley.

It was interesting living in the past this way. His memories were very clear. After all, it had not been that long ago — relative to his present time frame — that he had been there. He wondered if he and Sunitia had received the promised initiations in the golden pyramids and what that had done for their spiritual progress.

He wondered about his unborn daughter and what it would have been like to hold her and watch her grow up. He knew it had all happened — it was over and done with, many thousands of years ago. Yes, he knew all this, but as he preserved his memories and thoughts about it all, the deep sadness of not being with Sunitia was always present with him.

Toward the end of the month, the pain began to lessen somewhat, but his memories of her never receded even slightly. She was with him night and day.

He understood the ideal of letting go of all attachments and dwelling in inner freedom. He had always thought he had made good progress in moving toward this goal, and yet . . . , "Sunitia! O, my love, my life, Sunitia." Occasionally she stood in radiant beauty before his inner eye, smiling and welcoming. And when this happened, his heart broke all over again, as he reached out for her and she was not there, except in memory.

At the end of the four weeks, Simeon came to Thomas's home for his final scheduled visit and to receive Thomas's completed records. Thomas had spent the previous evening preparing for the close of his silence and seclusion time and for what he felt would be his most important meeting with Simeon. He prayed to be able to say clearly what was in his heart, that it be the right thing to say, and that Simeon would understand. He knew he was more prepared to face the future, no matter what it might bring.

"Good afternoon, Thomas."

"Good afternoon, Sir."

"Is your project finished and are you ready to turn it over to me?"

"Yes, it is done now and I'm ready to give it to you in its completed form, as you requested."

"Then let's sit in your garden and chat for a while."

At first, Simeon talked of how Thomas's fellow students were getting along in their time-travel adventures. He mentioned that they asked about him often and wondered about his prolonged absence.

"Do they know where I've been and what I've been doing?"

"I felt it best not to tell them more than that I had assigned you a special project that would keep you away from the Halls for a time."

"Thank you. I look forward to seeing them again."

"Shall we talk about Sunitia now?" Simeon asked.

Thomas replied, "I think I'm ready."

"Yes, I can feel that you've grown much stronger. You've learned a great deal about yourself during this challenging time. Your meditations have been very deep. I'm glad for you." Simeon paused for a few minutes.

"Thomas, I owe you an apology now."

Thomas was shocked to his core to hear this thought. He had never known Simeon to apologize to anyone for any reason. He couldn't imagine it! "Wha-a-at?" he stammered.

"Let me continue. In my own time-travel experiences and in helping many students over the years, I have never seen anyone react as dramatically as you have to what you experienced in your life with Sunitia. I finally realized that you may have run into something I have heard is possible, but that very rarely happens.

"It is said by those beings much wiser than I that there may be for each of us a 'soul mate,' or better stated, the other half of one's soul, dwelling in another body. It is thought that when a person is very close to living his or her last incarnation — when he is approaching final liberation and oneness with God — he is reunited with the soul who completes his essential nature. It is easy to misunderstand what is meant by this idea. It does not mean the union of two people in a human or romantic way. It is not necessarily a bond of husband and wife. This meeting can even be in vision, rather than in person."

Thomas was nearly breathless in contemplating this idea. "Sunitia?"

"It may be so." Simeon admitted. "Given the depth of what I see in your relationship with her, I'd say it is probable."

"Then I *can* be with her again soon, somehow?"

"Probably not in the way you are envisioning at the moment. The universal laws of time travel will not allow you to forsake your present body and move back into the lifetime you experienced with her in Descending Treta Yuga."

"Then what *can* I do to be with her? How can I be with her wherever she is now?" Thomas spoke aloud in his excitement.

"Thomas, please quiet your mind. All this is new to me, also. We must proceed carefully and slowly."

CHAPTER 17

The plan that Simeon now revealed to him was not entirely his own. Simeon was so deeply concerned about Thomas's overwhelming attachment to Sunitia that he had asked his superiors to meet with him in council.

Yes, Simeon had those to whom *he* looked for guidance. Until we reach final liberation and oneness with God, we continue to look for guidance from those who are more spiritually advanced than we ourselves. Simeon was a highly advanced soul, very close to the end of his spiritual journey; still, there were those who were even closer to the goal. It is a mark of wisdom to know when to ask for help from those more spiritually advanced.

"Thomas, I believe that you want to be finished with your worldly attachments and achieve final liberation — am I right about this?"

"Yes, Sir." There was a thoughtful pause. "Or at least I thought so until I met, or re-met, Sunitia. Now, I'm confused and unsure. I find myself unable to let go of my longing to be with her again. What shall I do?"

Simeon was pleased with Thomas's truthfulness and humility, and yet saddened by his obvious deep despair. Thomas was like a son to him, and the divine love he felt for him was strong and unconditional.

Simeon continued, "See what you think about this idea. We will continue with your time-travel training and experiences, but with some slight adjustments to the process of where/when you go. Will you agree to this?"

"Yes, if you think it best for me," Thomas thought carefully. "But what will be different?"

"It will be a specialized time travel in which you will be more an observer than a 'completely immersed' participant such as you were in your first experience."

"But why?" Thomas asked peevishly. "Is it because I blew it in my first experience of time travel?"

"No, not really." Simeon smiled. "Let me explain further. We feel it would be best for you to spend more time with Sunitia in a variety of situations and time frames."

Thomas gasped, aloud! This was completely unexpected. Despite his surprise, he had not missed the "we" that Simeon had used. "Who's 'we'?" he wondered. Simeon had always seemed to be such a loner.

Simeon smiled as he caught the thought. "Yes, Thomas. I, too, have my mentors. There are those who are more spiritually advanced than I, with whom I consult when there is something beyond my capacity to understand or solve. It is blissful to be in their presence — I enjoy having a challenging situation which calls for a conference with them. This I have done recently, on your behalf."

Thomas was not sure whether to be grateful or chagrined at being classified as a "challenging situation." He decided to exert great willpower and not react to these words. He remained silent, awaiting further instructions or explanations.

Knowing that Thomas was ready to hear him now, Simeon began to explain in thought pictures: "It is not ordinarily done this way for various good reasons, but there *is* a way to move through time as an observer rather than a participant. It's rather like watching a movie; you will be an outside observer of one of your past lives."

"So you think that if I fully experienced and participated in another part of a life with Sunitia, it would make me even more miserable than I am now?" Thomas knew his thoughts were tinged with regret, even anger. He didn't care!

"Thomas, there are many things you need to understand more fully about your connection with this soul you call Sunitia. Only *you* can go through this process and learn what you need to learn. Whether you learn through being completely immersed in a past life with her, or through experiencing that life as an observer, it really doesn't make that much difference. The lessons should be equally clear. May I suggest that we try once and see how you feel?"

Thomas asked and received time to take Simeon's plan into prayer and meditation. He felt confused and in some way belittled — as though he had failed a very important test.

Later, as he sat sadly by the river, he tried his best to go into inner silence, to return to that peaceful inner place that had seemed so easy for him to enter daily — before this recent turn of events. Eventually, and even as restless as Thomas felt his meditation time to have been, he intuitively felt that he knew the right answer.

Simeon was offering him the best solution available right now. If he refused it, he might lose all possible contact with the Sunitia-soul of past, present, or future. Even a non-first-hand contact with her would surely be better than no contact at all, in the same way that seeing a photograph or a movie of a lost loved one might be more a comfort than a deep pain.

Shaken to his core, and as miserable and lonely for Sunitia as he was, he still loved and trusted Simeon. He sensed that Simeon was doing his absolute best to help him through this karmic test.

The next day he returned to the Halls of Wisdom. He greeted his fellow students quietly. Their eyes held many questions, but they respected his privacy and said nothing except, "Welcome back, Thomas. We have missed you!"

To Simeon, he sent the private thought message, "I am ready for whatever is next, Sir. Let's get on with it as soon as possible."

CHAPTER 18

"As soon as possible" came only a few days later. Thomas was alone with Simeon in a "time-travel chapel." It was a small, lovely room, with a pyramid-shaped ceiling, quiet and lit by one fragrant candle on the altar. The colors of the walls and simple furnishings were various shades of blue and violet, soothing and uplifting.

At first they both sat cross-legged on deep blue mats, facing each other near the plain altar at the east side of the room. Thomas was given a thorough explanation of what would happen during this different version of time travel, and of what he could expect to feel.

Simeon explained how the process would differ from Thomas's first experience of time travel. This time he would go through something like hypnotism, but not the sort of hypnotism that could take away or weaken any of Thomas's free will. He would at all times be awake, aware, and in full possession of his faculties.

Simeon revealed that the time frame Thomas would soon experience had been difficult for him and, indeed, for all humans living then on this planet. He would be traveling to one and a half centuries before the birth of Christ, only 649 years before the end of Descending Kali Yuga — a time of darkness, ignorance, and great suffering worldwide.

Thomas had studied history in depth to prepare for his time-travel experiences. He had learned about the darkness of this time. The minds of most people were so unenlightened that such now unthinkable activities as violence, torture, murder, war were commonplace then. The very thought that he had lived through those "Dark Ages" (and that he had most probably done so repeatedly) was unsettling. He would *not* be entering a previous Treta Yuga, even in its descending phase!

Uneasy as he was at the thought of visiting Kali Yuga, Thomas was willing to endure anything to see Sunitia again — no matter the time or place. Simeon sensed Thomas's state of mind and was impressed with his bravery.

Simeon and Thomas then meditated together for several hours, both praying deeply for inner guidance in this unusual mission, the goal of which was to help Thomas understand the nature of his relationship to the soul he called Sunitia.

When it was time to begin, Simeon had a twinkle in his eye as he warned, "Thomas, one thing I need to tell you before we begin: Sunitia might not be recognizable to you at first."

"I know this, Sir. She was obviously in another body in that lifetime. Maybe she was not as beautiful. I really don't mind that at all. I probably didn't look so good in Kali Yuga either." He chuckled.

Simeon paused, and then presented Thomas with a stunning bit of news: "She was not a 'she' in that lifetime. This soul's name then was Caleb."

Thomas turned pale, trying hard to absorb the implications of what Simeon had just told him. Sunitia was not female then. Sunitia was. . . .

"Sunitia was a man then? I mean, I know that she has had many lives and been both male and female many times, but. . . ."

Here Thomas stopped, then projected his thought to Simeon. "I believe I understand now. She was a man and I was a woman — in the life I'm going to observe now — right?"

Simeon was silent.

"Yes, I see," Thomas went on. "We will be the same souls, closely knit with bonds of love, but in a reversed gender situation. Sounds fine to me. Let's go!"

Simeon remained silent. Thomas frowned at him. "What am I missing here?"

"Think about it for a moment, Thomas," Simeon said.

Slowly the light began to dawn in Thomas's mind. Stunned at the possibility, he asked, "Were we . . . were we . . . both men in that lifetime?"

"Yes," was Simeon's simple answer to Thomas. "Now, reflect carefully. Do you still want to experience this former lifetime?"

"Is this some sort of a trick?" Thomas was fighting disappointment and even exasperation.

"No trick, Thomas. It was then, and can be for you again, a lifetime of great learning — and surely a good one, if you open yourself to it. Do you want time to think it over?"

"But . . . Simeon, I mean, Sir, I mean. . . ." Thomas flailed about. "Are there no alternative lifetimes available to visit . . . another time, another place when we were together and we were . . . well, you know . . . ?"

"Yes, I know exactly what you are asking, Thomas. And the answer is no, not at this time. The decision has been made on this matter. Perhaps later." Simeon was kind but very firm in the way he gave Thomas this directive.

"Obviously, you need some time to get used to this idea. Shall we wait until tomorrow? Or do you need more time than that?"

"Uh, no, Sir. I mean, yes, Sir, I need some time; and tomorrow will be fine."

CHAPTER 19

It was a subdued Thomas who entered the same chapel the next day. He had slept very little, spending most of the night in prayer. Simeon was waiting for him, smiling and very pleased with his student. He knew Thomas's decision before Thomas had a chance to speak.

"Well done, Thomas! Shall we proceed?" No other communication was needed.

Again they meditated for a few hours; and again, when they were finished, Simeon asked Thomas if he had more questions.

"No, Sir. I am ready."

All night long he had wrestled with the thought of Sunitia and what it would be like to experience a life where they were together, probably as close friends, but not as lovers or as a married couple. He prayed deeply for clarity and guidance. As dawn came, he had become very calm with the reassurance that God was guiding this matter and that Simeon, his beloved teacher, along with the mysterious "others" who had made this decision, had only his best interests in mind.

Thomas became aware of floating high above a seemingly empty desert area. Whirlwinds of dust illuminated by a cruel, hot sun came and went below him. The year was 160 BC (540 Descending Kali Yuga) and the place was called Judea. The history and memories of this time and place began to filter back into Thomas's mind.

In the second century BC, the land of Judea, also called Israel, lay between Egypt and the Seleucid (Syrian) Empire to the north. The Seleucid Empire was strongly influenced by Greek society, having been formed from the dissolution of Alexander the Great's Greek empire. The Jewish culture of Judea had, at this time, been strongly subverted by Greek influence and was quickly losing its tradition and religious customs. Jewish religious feasts were banned, and circumcision was outlawed. Altars to Greek gods were set up everywhere, even in the great temple in Jerusalem, where a statue of Zeus had been placed. Possession of Jewish scriptures had been made a capital offence. Judaism seemed to be waning and on the point of disappearing altogether.

During this sad decline of Judaism, there arose a righteous Jew named Matthias Maccabbee. He and his five sons were forced to become outlaws and flee into the wilderness of Judea. Here they began successful guerilla warfare against the Seleucid dynasty. Eventually they were able to re-enter Jerusalem in triumph and ritually cleanse the Jewish Temple, reestablishing traditional Jewish worship in a large portion of Judea. The Jewish festival of Hanukkah was celebrated for many centuries after this event, to commemorate the Maccabbeans' miraculous victory over their powerful enemies.

Thomas noticed that the barren desert he had been hovering over was not completely empty. Now he saw that this place had recently been a battlefield. It was littered with broken spears, helmets, shields, and other implements of warfare that Thomas began to remember with a shudder of horror. War! In its ugliest form.

Thomas had no firsthand experience of warfare of this sort. Mantric wars he understood, but not *this* kind of war, with blood and gore, and the screams of the injured and dying echoing around him. For this was not only Kali Yuga, it was the darkest part of the whole 24,000-year yuga cycle — it was *Descending* Kali Yuga! All that had been gained in previous higher ages had been lost. Most people's consciousness held only a dim flickering light. Everything was difficult! Everything was gross!

Thomas was tempted to withdraw and go elsewhere. But he knew he had been drawn to this place for a good reason. He was certain that an earlier version of himself must be nearby, even though this scene felt deserted except for sad vibrations of fallen soldiers.

Looking around more carefully, Thomas noticed that at the far edge of the desert plain there was a low, rugged mountain range, pocked with what appeared to be caves. Attracted to one cave in particular, he found himself at its entrance. Peering inside and blinking at the contrast between the heat and brilliant sunlight outside and the cool dimness inside this cave, Thomas began gradually to perceive two people lying on the ground at the back of the cave. Venturing inside, he could hear their voices and know their thoughts.

"Caleb," another Thomas said loudly, shaking the wounded Maccabbeean soldier. "Caleb! You must not die. You can't die now. The battle is over. We won! It was a great victory. Caleb, speak to me!"

Thomas lifted a skin bag of water to the parched lips of his best friend. "Drink!" he commanded.

"Please drink," he said more softly, through tears he was doing his best to hold back. Maccabbean warriors did not cry!

The Treta Yuga Thomas observed the Kali Yuga Thomas with interest. He was astonished at the similarity in their appearance. And they seemed even to have the same name. He realized the wisdom in Simeon's insistence that he not "become" an earlier version of himself. Traveling as an observer, he could remain slightly more detached and thereby be able to observe what was going on more clearly, rather than being totally immersed in the incarnation, not even aware that he was *in* another lifetime.

Although he understood that the Kali Yuga Thomas and his dearest friend, Caleb, did not know he was there with them, Thomas did not feel like an intruder. How could he be intruding on his own life? Anyway, he was sure that there were lessons to be learned here, and Simeon had insisted that he learn them.

Dim, lost memories of this lifetime began to percolate into his present consciousness and with them the pain of this moment became more real.

Thomas and Caleb had grown up together in Jerusalem, the best of friends from birth. They had been born in the same year, to families who were close friends. Two years ago and before the most recent Maccabbean battle had been fought, Caleb had married Thomas's favorite younger sister, Sarah. It was a love match, even though it had been arranged by the two Jewish families. Sarah was now seven months pregnant with their first child.

Recently, much to their family's unhappiness, Caleb and Thomas had been caught up in the fervor of the Maccabbean fight for religious integrity and freedom from the increasing incursions of their enemies to the north. They had joined the guerilla forces and fought side by side with those great Judaic heroes, the Maccabbee brothers — striving to free their country. It was a glorious time for these brave young men and it cemented their already strong friendship.

They had fought side by side in several battles, but the most recent battle had been different. True, they had won, but Thomas had been knocked unconscious toward the close of the battle. Regaining partial consciousness, he found himself being dragged off the battlefield by Caleb. Various skirmishes were still happening around them, but Caleb paid no attention. He was determined to drag Thomas to safety before returning to the battle himself. Thomas smiled at this memory. He knew he would have done the same for his friend.

The bonds of love between them were strong — stronger than in any other relationship they had in this lifetime. They loved their parents and other siblings. Certainly their family ties were important. Yes, they loved the Maccabbee heroes and fought bravely for their cause. Caleb was obviously besotted with his young wife. But with Thomas and Caleb it was different — one could start a sentence and the other would finish it. They knew each other's thoughts. They anticipated each other's actions. They never spoke of their closeness to each other — it would not have been seemly between young men of their times, especially the strong soldiers they were; but they sometimes felt as though they were one soul in two bodies. They were inseparable and had been from birth, and now, it seemed, perhaps in death also.

For now Caleb seemed to be holding on to life by a thread. Three days ago, just before they had reached the mouth of the cave, with Thomas beginning to be able to struggle along without as much aid from Caleb, a lone Seleucidian warrior had surprised them both, sprang up from behind a desert bush and screamed, "Die, Maccabbee!"

With that cry, he plunged his sword into Caleb's side and fled. Thomas tried to chase him, but after only a few steps, he fell and passed out again for a time. When he came back to consciousness, night had fallen and he could hear the cries of jackals and other scavengers of the night.

"Caleb? Caleb!" he cried.

By starlight, he saw his fallen friend close by. Dead? Surely not!

Caleb was still alive, but barely. Struggling with all his remaining energy, Thomas carried Caleb into the cave and tried to care for his deadly wound as best he could. But Thomas had been a soldier long enough to know that too much blood had been lost, and that Caleb surely couldn't live much longer.

Thomas began to pray out loud a simple Jewish prayer for the repose of both their souls. "Yahweh, we commend our souls back into Your loving arms, from whence we came. Hear, O Israel, the Lord our God is One. He is One. Amen, Amen, Amen."

Alone in the cave with Caleb, Thomas knew that the great Maccabbeean battle was completely over. The dead and injured had been taken away. Weakened from his own head injury and lack of food, Thomas was not sure that he himself could stay alive very much longer. He didn't have the strength to go for help from the victorious army, though it was not far away.

And so Treta Yuga Thomas observed this scene now, with deep compassion and understanding. He knew with certainty that they had both died there, friends, soul brothers, companions to the end.

Over and over, Thomas sang his prayer. Eventually, his voice weakening, his prayer changed to: *"Barukh atah Adonai Eloheinu melekh ha'olam, dayan ha-emet:* Blessed are You, Lord our God, King of the universe, the True Judge. Amen" — a Jewish prayer for the newly dead. Caleb's shallow breathing had ceased. Morning revealed the two friends lying side by side, their spirits departed to the astral world, there to rest, renew, and review this past life — and eventually to ready themselves for a new lifetime.

Thomas now found himself resting on a soft blue-violet mat, looking into Simeon's beautiful silver eyes. "Is it over?" he said.

Simeon nodded and helped Thomas sit up.

"I thought I had died and . . . Caleb, too."

"You did, of course — both of you."

"Of course," said Thomas, slowly re-orienting himself to his present surroundings. "Yes, we died, but. . . . Oh, the love, the closeness, the oneness — that could never die, could it?"

Simeon only smiled and gave Thomas a cup of cool water to drink.

CHAPTER 20

Thomas went home for rest and reflection. He returned to speak with Simeon late the next afternoon.

"Well?" was Simeon's simple opening query.

"Well, I wasn't in Kali Yuga very long, was I? And I didn't feel as deeply involved as I did in my first experience. I understand that we planned it that way; nevertheless, I feel that I learned important lessons." Thomas replied.

"Tell me what you learned."

"I learned that 542 Descending Kali Yuga was not a pleasant place to be." They both chuckled.

Thomas went on, "I learned that love between two people can be very deep, even if it is not romantic love. The love I felt for Caleb in that lifetime in Judea was very strong! I would have given my life for him a thousand times over, and I know he would have done the same for me. It didn't matter at all to me that he was not a woman or even a part of my blood family. But I realize now that it never had occurred to me that love for a friend and love for one's spouse could be equal."

Thomas paused for a few breaths, and then plunged in again. "This brings up a question, however. What is love? The love I feel for Sunitia and the love I felt for Caleb — they seem equal to me now; yet they don't feel quite the same somehow. It *is* obviously still love in both cases, right? What does this mean? And when Caleb and I died in that lifetime, where did the love go?"

Simeon sighed. His star pupil obviously needed to go to "love school" (again) for some remedial work. Simeon knew they'd been over this basic subject before in many previous classes, over the course of many years. He also knew that studying an abstract concept like love, and experiencing what it really feels like firsthand, are two very different things.

"Thomas, do you remember a beautiful song called 'What Is

Love?' that I taught you when you were a child?"

"I think so," said Thomas.

"Let's sing it together now; and please listen carefully to the words."

> What is love? Is it only ours,
> Or does love whisper in the flowers?
>> Surely we, children of this world,
> Could not love by our own powers.[©]

They sang the song together several times. It was pleasant, sitting together in the quiet grove of trees where they had agreed to meet, singing with soft voices while watching the sun go down.

Thomas mused to himself, "It's interesting how a song like this, so simple and sweet, can go right to the core of my heart and reveal a world beyond the intellect. I'm always trying to figure things out, when the answer is right inside me, like a forgotten song."

Simeon replied to Thomas's thoughts, "Truth is simple, everything else is complex. True love is never ours to have or own. We may feel energy that we call love, but if it doesn't come from a Divine Source, flowing through us unobstructed by desires or attachments, then it is not Divine Love; it is therefore imperfect — polluted by likes, dislikes, wants, and needs.

"Human love, generally speaking, is held in bondage by attachments. It always ends in sorrow and disappointment; it makes many promises but keeps few of them. Perhaps this sounds harsh, but Thomas, you *must* learn this lesson. There is *no* pure, perfect, completely satisfying love except Divine Love. The power to love others, to love yourself, to love anything at all is not your own. It is a gift from God, which can flow through you, but it is *not your own!*"

"Then what do I feel for Sunitia if it is not true love?"

"It is many things: attachment, desire, attraction, and a conditional love which says, 'I love you *if* you behave in a certain way; but if you don't, perhaps I won't love you as much.'"

Thomas began to feel stubborn. "I don't think Sunitia could ever disappoint me! I certainly could *never* love her less, just because of the way she acted."

"Shall we put that to the test?" Simeon asked.

"What do you mean?" Thomas said, alarmed at the sheer force of Simeon's challenging tone of thought.

Simeon continued, "I think it's time for you to visit a different part of Kali Yuga."

CHAPTER 21

Simon revealed that the next year Thomas was to visit was 1070 AD (566 Ascending Kali Yuga), 570 years past the lowest part of Kali Yuga, another truly dark time in this cycle of the yugas.

"Well," he mused, "at least this time I'll be in a time frame that is moving upward rather than downward." Thomas was trying to insert a little humor into the conversation. Simeon did not seem amused.

"Don't push it, Thomas," Simeon replied. "Perhaps there are worse times or places to have been incarnated than in Kali Yuga, but I think you'll find your soul had plenty to deal with during this particular lifetime in Normandy.

"Hm-m-m-m, Normandy? Was my name Thomas again?

"No."

"Well, at least that's new and different. Okay, what was my name in 1070 AD in Normandy?" Thomas was being a little sarcastic and willful. "No, let me guess. . . ." Thomas tried to remember some details of his ancient history lesson.

Thomas continued, "In 1070 AD Normandy, though geographically a part of France, was being ruled by William I., otherwise known as William the Conqueror as he was known after his 1066 conquest of England. Thus, William I was the ruler of both England and Normandy at that time. Am I correct?"

Simeon was silent.

"All right, then I'd guess my name was William? Edward? Henry? Robert Curthose? Lanfranc?" Thomas was smugly congratulating himself for remembering some of the more prominent names of that time period and geographical location.

"Try again," Simeon was patient.

Thomas realized he was fresh out of historic names, so he simply said, "Simeon, I'm sorry. I really don't have a clue. Tell me."

"How about Gwendolyn?" Simeon smiled, somewhat impishly.

"Gwendolyn! Gwendolyn? Gwendolyn who? Who was she — who, who . . . I mean was she, me, or who . . . was me a she . . . or who, who . . . ?"

"Thomas!" Simeon was shaking with silent laughter at his student's confusion. "Your grammar is deteriorating rapidly and you sound like a hoot owl — who-o, who, hoo-o-o-o!"

Chagrined, Thomas realized that in this next time-travel sequence, he was going to have a new experience; he would be observing one of his past lives as a *female*. He had always understood that changing gender from one life to another was possible, actually probable! But still, now that the time had come to experience being a woman it was difficult to get used to the concept.

"I hope I'm very beautiful, then," he thought with amusement, "and that Sunitia is . . . perhaps a dashing and handsome soldier again, as she was in that life as Caleb." Thomas was fantasizing about another wonderful love affair between himself and Sunitia, even if their roles were reversed — still there would be the romance, the love, the joy . . . ah-h-h, yes!

Simeon was not laughing at all. "Thomas, Sunitia's name in that time was Jeanne-Louise. She was your daughter. And yes, she was fair of face." Here Simeon paused. "But I will say no more right now. It's time for you to observe this lifetime on your own."

Thomas sighed, knowing he would learn no more from his teacher just now.

Gwendolyn and Jeanne-Louise? Mother and daughter? With no further hesitation he declared, "Simeon, I think I understand, and I am ready to go."

The truth was that he understood very little and didn't particularly care that much. He was secretly very happy to be once again close to this fair-of-face Sunitia, no matter what his (or her) relationship to her might have been in that long-ago lifetime in Normandy, in a dark, violent Kali Yuga. He simply wanted to see her as a female again.

CHAPTER 22

⌒⁊⌒

Gwendolyn was a highly placed servant, a maid to Matilda, queen of Normandy and England, and the wife of William I, who is well known to history as William the Conqueror.

Gwendolyn knew how very blessed she was to be in such a position. Her mother had been Matilda's nurse and early governess. When Gwendolyn's mother had died at a young age, Princess Matilda insisted that her nurse's daughter remain in the court as her playmate and friend, though nominally as her chambermaid. The two girls were close in age, and they shared the secrets all young girls have.

After the great conquest of 1066, Matilda became queen of both England and Normandy. Life was exciting, though dangerous and ever uncertain, even for a queen. Matilda was, at this time, especially glad for Gwendolyn's company. They lived primarily in Normandy, in one of William's safer palaces, while William lived across the channel in England, trying to consolidate his newly forming and tumultuous kingdom there. Matilda loved her husband and missed him very much, but she had her sons and daughters, courtiers and friends, and of course, her dear friend Gwendolyn to keep her company.

Life was as good as it could get for two women of that violent age. Warfare was constant and disease was rampant. Living conditions were marginal, even for those with wealth. Religion didn't help very much, as the Catholic Church was also in disarray.

Thomas was unhappy to see what he looked like as Gwendolyn, chambermaid to Matilda. Gwendolyn had never been a pretty girl. She was short, stocky, and red-faced. But she had a nice smile and was kind and giving to all. Gwendolyn was not intelligent, and though as Matilda's childhood friend she had been given opportunities to become literate, she never learned to read or write. She couldn't see the use for books or learning.

Her mother had trained Gwendolyn well as a servant of the royal court. Gwendolyn helped with birthing and raising Matilda's sons and daughters, and was especially fond of her baby daughter Cecily.

Then a dark cloud passed over Gwendolyn's life, a year after Matilda gave birth to Cecily. Gwendolyn came to Matilda and admitted sadly that she was pregnant. Matilda was shocked and angry at this, especially when Gwendolyn, with whom she had shared all her deepest secrets, refused to reveal the father's name.

Gwendolyn, on her knees, tearful and fearful, begged Matilda not to cast her out of the royal court. For where could a disgraced servant woman with an illegitimate child go? What could she do?

Matilda, though not without faults, was nevertheless a compassionate woman. When she asked William his advice on the matter, he gave her leave to make this decision on her own. He would not interfere. But his advice to her was a quote from the Holy Scriptures of those times: "Do unto others as you would have them do unto you."

Thus Gwendolyn was allowed to stay with Matilda's inner circle of servants. She soon gave birth to her own daughter, Jeanne-Louise. Almost from birth, it was clear that Jeanne-Louise was very beautiful. Only a year younger than Cecily, she soon became a "little sister" to Princess Cecily; it seemed like a continuation of the relationship between their mothers.

Jeanne-Louise never really accepted the idea that she was the daughter of a servant, and therefore a servant herself. Cecily insisted, from the beginning, that her stunningly beautiful "little sister" be given every gift and privilege that was given to her. Matilda had matters of state on her mind, not to mention the challenges of raising her four boisterous sons, Robert Curthose, Richard, William Rufus, and Henry. And Gwendolyn was simply grateful to be allowed to have her daughter close by, as she served her queen.

As Jeanne-Louise grew older, her physical beauty seemed to increase in direct opposition to her character traits. She was selfish, haughty, and unkind, especially to her mother. As sometimes happens in a relationship of this sort, the more badly she treated her mother, the more Gwendolyn loved her, indulged her, and shielded her from the increasing disfavor of others in Queen Matilda's retinue.

Cecily loved Jeanne-Louise, too, and did her part to spoil her, never allowing a single negative word to be spoken about Jeanne-Louise in her presence. Jeanne-Louise was her living doll. And Cecily was, unfortunately, somewhat weak to begin with. As they grew older, Jeanne-Louise came to hold the reins of that relationship firmly in her hands.

Thomas observed all this as a quickly passing panorama. He didn't particularly like himself as Gwendolyn and was shocked to see what an annoying, ill-mannered brat his beloved Sunitia (Jeanne-Louise) was in this lifetime. As much as he loved her still, many times he wanted to smack her hard as he watched her self-centeredness grow stronger and stronger. And worse yet, she got away with it.

How besotted Gwendolyn was with her lovely, strong-willed daughter and how easily she overlooked all her glaring faults. Thomas could understand Gwendolyn's attitude, but was greatly disturbed by it. He had never thought of Sunitia except as of the best, dearest, loveliest person who ever lived. Now he was observing a new side of his beloved. How had she come to be so spoiled and unpleasant?

Time passed, the girls grew into young women, and Matilda and William began to confer over an important matter. Royal princesses in those times were given in marriage for political reasons, to help their fathers build strong alliances with rulers of other countries, and thus strengthen their own power.

Their daughter Agatha had been betrothed to Alphonse of Spain to help forge a critically important alliance between Spain and England. Now it was Cecily's turn.

Cecily had watched the anguish that her sister Agatha had gone through and was saddened by the depths of Agatha's desire not to have to live in Spain and be married to a stranger, albeit the King of Spain.

Agatha had never been able to understand that her royal parents' love for her must be tempered with the needs of the country they ruled. Thus she resisted their decision completely, so much so that history tells us she died a virgin. Princess Agatha was found dead on her knees in prayer on the ship carrying her to Spain to marry Alphonse. She had prayed for death in preference to this politically important marriage.

Cecily confided to Jeanne-Louise her deep sadness about the plight of her older sister and her fears for her own future. Princess Cecily was now of marriageable age and her father, King William, would be looking for a suitable marriage alliance. The wily, self-serving Jeanne-Louise began to see here the perfect opportunity to interfere and promote her own cause in the court.

A t this point Thomas began to observe his former life as Gwendolyn in "real time" and not as a quickly passing "movie" of what had brought them to this moment. Seeing the fifteen-year-old Jeanne-Louise took his breath away. She looked very much like Sunitia, perhaps even more beautiful. He watched her with love, but also with increasing dismay as he saw her gleefully reveal to Gwendolyn that she had talked the sixteen-year-old Princess Cecily into running away to join a convent.

"Jeanne-Louise!" Gwendolyn was deeply shocked. "This is treason! Cecily is a royal princess. She cannot disobey her parents. You must not do this thing. Her father, our King and Protector, needs to offer her in marriage to a prince in order to forge another important European alliance just as he tried to do with Princess Agatha."

"But Mother, Cecily doesn't want to marry some stranger and become isolated and lonely as a princess in some foreign land with strange people, languages, food, and customs." Jeanne-Louise flipped her radiant golden curls and smiled saucily at her homely mother.

Gwendolyn's heart sank to her feet.

Thomas was carefully watching Jeanne-Louise/Sunitia. How could she behave like this? Cruel and disrespectful to her loving mother (himself!), scheming against the wishes of her King, a noble and wise man who along with Matilda had been very good to her — how could this be? She was not acting at all like the person he knew and loved. What could have happened to make her behave in this way now?

Thomas knew instinctively that disaster was just around the corner for Jeanne-Louise/Sunitia, and by extension, for himself as Gwendolyn. But, of course, he was powerless to stop the events of his past lifetime. He could only observe and learn from what had happened to him and Sunitia, in the dark times of Kali Yuga.

So many questions! So few answers! What could be motivating Jeanne-Louise to give this treacherous advice to Cecily? Cecily didn't seem to be a particularly religious girl. A convent would surely be a harsh and unhappy place for her to live for the rest of her life.

Then the answers began to form in his mind. Jeanne-Louise was living in a fantasy world in which she hoped to take Cecily's place in the king and queen's favors. She had not figured out exactly how she would do that — how she could become the one given in marriage to a royal prince — even a duke would do. But surely, with Cecily tucked safely away in a quiet religious life, her star could begin to shine without obstruction. She had full confidence that her beauty and intelligence would finally be recognized and honored. Such were her dreams, and she would do whatever it took to bring them to fruition!

Gwendolyn began to plead, cry, and beg her beloved daughter to desist from encouraging Cecily in this mad idea, but to no avail.

Finally, with heavy heart, Gwendolyn knew what she must do. She must tell Matilda and through her, King William, what was going on. And Gwendolyn, soft of heart and mind, could not hide her plans from her beloved daughter.

Thomas now saw Jeanne-Louise, his beauteous one, his

soulmate, slip poison into Gwendolyn's food to viciously murder her own mother in order to keep her from revealing this scheme. He watched Gwendolyn die a horrible death.

Jeanne-Louise continued with her plan to get Cecily into a nunnery. She masterminded Cecily's escape from the palace and helped her gain entry into the Holy Trinity Convent in Caen, France.

Cecily entered the convent in secret and prepared to take vows of complete renunciation. At that time she sent her "faithful friend," Jeanne-Louise, back to the court. This, of course, was Jeanne-Louise's dearest wish. Her scheme had worked very well so far, and now all that remained was to return to Matilda and William's court and let her ravishingly beautiful face and forceful personality work its magic on them, as it had on so many others. Life was moving along perfectly for her now.

However, Queen Matilda did not greet her cordially, as Jeanne-Louise had expected. Matilda had been suspicious about Gwendolyn's death almost immediately; and unbeknownst to anyone, she had asked her personal physician to examine Gwendolyn's body. The physician told Matilda that her body exhibited the signs of an ingestion of some sort of powerful poison.

Also, while Jeanne-Louise was making her way back from France, Cecily had discovered that she missed her dearest friend very much. Now she wished she had told Jeanne-Louise to remain with her in the convent. She asked her mother to send Jeanne-Louise back to be with her as soon as possible.

And so it came to be that when Jeanne-Louise arrived back at the palace, Queen Matilda was very cold to her and, shortly thereafter, ordered her to return to Caen to serve her daughter in the convent for the rest of her life.

Only then did Jeanne-Louise realize that as a servant and a friendless orphan, life would offer nothing better for her if she didn't follow the Queen's orders. Jeanne-Louise soon found herself back in France, head shaven, beautiful clothing and jewels taken away, the servant of a nun in a cold, stone convent in France. Interestingly enough, Princess Cecily came to love life in the convent, and found her place in the heart of the Church. She eventually became the Abbess of Holy Trinity Convent.

Jeanne-Louise grew very bitter as the years went by. She lost her beauty and her health. Miserable and virtually alone, she also had to live with the guilt of having killed her own mother.

Thomas watched Jeanne-Louise die very young, sick in her body and mind. Her spirit seemed crushed. It was heartbreaking to observe.

CHAPTER 23

_～qc～_

"Simeon, that life didn't turn out very well," Thomas thought ruefully. "I mean, it was not an easy life for me, was it?"

"Remember, Thomas, what Paramhansa Yogananda, the great master of yoga whose life we have studied carefully, once said: 'An easy life is not a victorious life.'"

It was a stretch for Thomas to see how Gwendolyn's life could be called a "victorious life." But he saw that, although it had not been easy for him/her, he had learned some valuable lessons while being Gwendolyn.

Thomas went on, "And Kali Yuga was terrible on every level! How could anyone stand to live in that time?"

Simeon seemed grave. "It _was_ very hard, you are right! As you know, most people didn't live long in Kali Yuga, those dark, dark ages. In Treta Yuga, we live, on an average, three or four times longer."

"I'm getting a feeling for the dramatically different ways of living and thinking among the different yuga cycles!" Thomas thought wryly.

"Thomas, get some rest now. We'll talk about Gwendolyn and Jeanne-Louise later. Meditate on what you have learned."

After a few days of rest and introspection, Thomas attempted to contact Simeon to see when they could meet. He had one burning question to ask about Sunitia/Jeanne-Marie. Simeon transmitted the thought to him that he had been called to another galaxy for a few days and that Thomas would need to wait.

"Go and talk with your fellow students until I return. Tell them what you are learning in your time travels. I'm sure they'll be interested."

Thomas did as he was instructed and went to visit his class-mates. It was a joyful and interesting reunion. Many of his classmates had themselves been having interesting time-travel experiences and were eager to share what they had learned and experienced in other time frames.

But despite Simeon's instructions, Thomas was mostly silent; he listened to their stories, smiling and making appropriate comments. But he didn't feel ready to speak of the deeply moving and emotional experiences he had been having recently. He felt "raw" and knew he was still painfully confused.

Most of his friends didn't notice — they were quite full of their own experiences and eager to talk at length about their adventures in faraway times and places.

However, perhaps because she and Thomas had worked together closely during their photism concerts, Sabella did notice his silence and the uncharacteristic aura of sadness around him.

When she got the chance, she asked if she could speak with him alone. They strolled through a meadow for a while, not saying anything, just enjoying the beauty of the day.

Finally she ventured a quiet thought in his direction: "Thomas, what is going on with you? You are very quiet and you seem sorrowful. Can you tell me? Please don't feel you have to, but as your friend, I'd love to help you if I can."

Thomas was touched by her sweet sincerity and kindness.

"Sabella, I very much appreciate your concern. I have been having a rough time with some of my experiences in past yugas. It has not been what I expected, and I am troubled at the ways in which I have reacted to what happened to me."

Sabella made no comment in thought or speech, though she was very curious to know more. She felt that her own time-travel experiences had matured her in many ways.

Thomas finally decided that Simeon must have had a reason to encourage him to share with his fellow students. Perhaps sharing with Sabella would fulfill this commission.

"I will tell you the highlights, but I must ask for your complete confidence in this matter."

"Thomas, I will never think or breathe a word of it to anyone!" Her eyes shown kindly and he knew she was truthful and sincere.

At the end of his long narration (she had interrupted from time to time with questions — which he actually found helpful in processing what he was learning) he noticed tears in her eyes.

Brushing them aside, she said, "I am humbled that you would tell me all this. I can see that it is deeply personal, and I understand your sadness a little better. Thank you."

"I feel better too — lighter and freer somehow. Let's go for a swim!"

Laughing like children, they sprinted to the nearby river and swam, played, and rested for several hours, speaking no more about time travel. For the first time in a long while, Thomas let go of his mental and emotional burdens and enjoyed the here and now.

CHAPTER 24

Simeon contacted him upon his return and was happy to see that Thomas looked calmer; he seemed refreshed in body, mind, and spirit.

"What was your burning question, my son?"

"It doesn't seem quite so 'burning' now, but here it is: What horrible thing must I have done to Jeanne-Louise/Sunitia in some previous lifetime to have her murder me in that lifetime? We were so very happy and so much in love in that first Descending Treta Yuga life that I experienced with her."

"Do you really want to know, Thomas?"

"I think so. I mean, shouldn't I *need* to know about this?"

"Sri Yukteswar," Simeon transmitted to Thomas, "whom you remember from our course called 'The Lives of the Great Ones,' was quoted in his disciple Yogananda's spiritual classic, *Autobiography of a Yogi*, as saying, 'Forget the past. The vanished lives of all men are dark with many shames. Human conduct is ever unreliable until anchored in the Divine. Everything in future will improve if you are making a spiritual effort now.'"

Thomas became uneasy. "Sir, I don't understand! Is visiting other lifetimes to learn about myself a worthless thing to do? Should I forget the past and just work on my spiritual life, on my meditation practices?"

"Our past karma, the result of our past actions, has great power over us — greater than most people realize. But remember that Sri Yukteswar offered these wise words in response to new students who occasionally expressed doubts regarding their own worthiness to engage in yoga-meditation practice."

Simeon continued, "Time-travel skills are given to us in Treta Yuga to supplement the work we do in our meditations and spiritual practices. Time travel is simply another tool for learning about ourselves and letting go of the past. It may be less effective than what can be accomplished in deep Kriya Yoga meditation practice, which is the best possible technique for working out our karma quickly and efficiently. But it has its place.

"Should you want to know what horrible thing you did to cause yourself, as Gwendolyn, to be murdered by your own daughter? That is completely up to you. If you really want to know the cause-effect relationship in that event, we can arrange for you to see it in detail."

Simeon paused and gave Thomas an enigmatic smile while he raised his eyebrows in a questioning expression.

"Let me think about that and get back to you, Sir."

"Fine, my son. We are in no rush. Pray and meditate; you'll know what to do."

CHAPTER 25

Thomas was fairly sure that his curiosity would get the better of him. It might be a sign of his lack of spiritual progress to want to know the *true reasons* for everything, but he decided to quit being concerned about this "fault," if it was one. The next day he told Simeon that he definitely did want to know the past-life events that had led Jeanne-Louise to murder Gwendolyn.

"What would you think might be a reason, Thomas?" Simeon thought quietly.

"I'd guess that in a previous lifetime I took *her* life? And *that* karma had to be balanced in a subsequent lifetime?"

"Dead right!" Simeon laughed out loud at his pun. "I respect your decision, so please prepare yourself now and we'll see what happened to set up your untimely death."

"Before we start, Simeon, may I ask if I was a woman in the lifetime that I'm going to see/experience right now? I must admit I don't really care for this 'sex changing' thing."

"Get used to it!" Simeon showed little pity for his student's agitation. "We've all changed countless times — our gender, culture, race, even our galaxy. Remember that. . . ."

Thomas interrupted somewhat impatiently. "Yes, yes, I know. My soul and all souls have no gender, personality, culture, race, time frame, or planetary home."

Simeon did not chide his student for his curt interruption. He knew that Thomas still had much to learn, but he was glad that Thomas had the courage and willingness to move forward in learning whatever he needed to learn, even if he was confused or frightened.

Thomas was, indeed, a woman again. She was living at the time of Jesus Christ (about 33 AD or 733 Descending Kali Yuga), forward in time from his life in Judea as a Maccabbean soldier.

He began to watch his life unfold as Abigail, the haughty wife of a very rich and powerful Pharisee. Their home stood on a high hill in Jerusalem, close to the great temple of Israel.

At the time, Abigail was very disturbed by the actions of her husband, Nicodemus. Nicodemus was a great scholar, judge, and one of the Pharisees, the religious rulers of the Jews. Though the Jews were under Roman rule and were essentially a conquered and subservient nation at that time, the Romans wisely let the Jewish religious leaders maintain a level of power and influence — as long, of course, as it didn't interfere with Roman law and power.

Abigail loved her life of wealth and status. She was raising her three children to enjoy that life in the same ways she did. She had dozens of servants and treated them well, though firmly.

Their lives were going along quite well until another ragtag, would-be Messiah had started hanging around Jerusalem. This man, Jesus, was causing an unusually big stir, especially among the poor and the lower classes. One evening Nicodemus confided to Abigail that he had been listening (in secret) to this Jesus person teach. He told her that he felt strongly that Jesus was truly a "man of God," perhaps even the long-anticipated Jewish Messiah.

Abigail was horrified at his words. "Nicodemus, my dear husband, you must *not* be seen in the company of this imposter! Nor should you listen to his words at all. My dearest women friends, wives of your fellow Pharisees, have told me all about him. To agree with his teachings would mean political and religious disaster for you, and a complete loss of status for our family."

Nicodemus was sad to hear his wife's words — he had been hoping she might accompany him to hear Jesus, for he knew that it was almost impossible for anyone to listen to him and not be deeply moved, perhaps even changed forever. Now he knew his hope was out of the question, and that he should be completely quiet on the subject in the future.

The conversation between Nicodemus and Abigail was overheard by one of Abigail's maids, a sweet girl from a poor, distant province called Nazareth. (Servants in those days often managed to overhear family conversations they were not meant to hear — for doing so was sometimes a survival technique.)

Abigail's servant's name was Miriam, but Thomas, the observer, instantly recognized her as Sunitia. Unbeknownst to Abigail or Nicodemus, Miriam was a cousin of this man named Jesus. She had known him as a child and loved him as a friend and eventually as her spiritual teacher. For this reason, whenever she could, she went to the places Jesus stayed or taught. She knew without question that he was the long-awaited Messiah. She listened eagerly to the stories of his many great miracles and had even witnessed a few of them herself.

Eventually Miriam gathered her courage and spoke to Nicodemus. Nicodemus knew who she was, of course, but had previously paid little attention to her. He had given Abigail complete control in managing their home and servants, for he believed that she was very competent in this role.

Miriam had taken care that no one else was around at that time. Abigail, she knew, was visiting her sister in a different part of Jerusalem. "Sir," Miriam began, "I am a cousin of Jesus and consider him to be my spiritual teacher and also the promised Messiah. I know that you admire him and listen to his wise words, as I do. I beg you, if you see me at any gathering where Jesus is present, please do not tell your wife about it. I do not think she would be pleased to know of my dedication to him."

Nicodemus was very surprised; in a way, he was delighted to hear he had a "confederate" in his own household. Promising to keep her secret and extracting her promise that she would keep his growing admiration for Jesus a secret also, Nicodemus left their home to attend to business matters.

Abigail and Nicodemus almost came to blows when she learned not only that he had *not* stopped seeing Jesus, but that after Jesus was crucified like the common criminal she was now sure he was, Nicodemus offered part of their family burial place for Jesus's body to rest. And if that wasn't outrageous enough, he had also purchased a very expensive mixture of myrrh and aloes, about a hundred-pound weight, with which he, with his own hands, helped to prepare the body as prescribed by Jewish burial practices. Nicodemus's actions were completely unacceptable to Abigail!

Now the rumors were circulating wildly that his body was no longer resting in their tomb (who knew what *that* meant?), and Abigail was struggling to "save face" among her many friends, who certainly had heard by now that her husband was connected to this terrible imposter.

During this time, another of Abigail's serving maids, infamous among fellow servants for her ambitious ways, was scheming to displace Miriam as Abigail's favorite personal maid. It was hard to keep secrets in a house full of servants, and she had learned of Miriam's devotion to Jesus.

Knowing of Abigail's great hatred of Jesus, the wicked woman told Abigail Miriam's secret. To assure her promotion in the household, she added a little "spice" to her story, telling her mistress with great relish that not only was Miriam part of the Jesus group, but that she was also having an affair with Nicodemus.

Abigail didn't hesitate for a moment. She called Miriam to her and confronted her with this information. Miriam admitted to following Jesus — what else could she do? But she truthfully and tearfully denied having a love affair with Nicodemus.

Abigail refused to believe her. In her rage, she wouldn't listen to another word from Miriam. Later that evening she crept into Miriam's sleeping quarters and stabbed her to death. When the death was discovered, the ambitious servant — the one who had spread the false rumors about Miriam — knew very well who had committed the murder. But she claimed to have seen a strange and unknown man coming and going from Miriam's room nightly, and had heard them arguing the very night Miriam was killed. With the murder thus "solved," she was immediately promoted to take Miriam's place as Abigail's primary serving-maid.

CHAPTER 26

Thomas watched his sweet Sunitia/Miriam die a horrible death at "his" (Abigail's) hands. He perceived Miriam's thoughts as she died: "I know that Jesus taught us to forgive everyone, but I shall never forgive Abigail for murdering me in cold blood, on the basis of a false rumor — she never even bothered to try to find out the truth. She was punishing her husband, who deserved no punishment, through me. I will have my vengeance upon this wicked, wicked woman somehow, someday!"

As he spoke with Simeon about what he had seen of that long-ago lifetime, Thomas seemed again dazed and dismayed. "So Miriam, who was Jeanne-Louise in Ascending Kali Yuga, and who was my Sunitia in Descending Treta Yuga — was murdered by Abigail who became Gwendolyn, who was me at the time of William the Conqueror. That karmic action in the time of Christ caused Jeanne-Louise (Sunitia) to kill Gwendolyn (me), her mother in that later lifetime. Have I got that straight, Sir?"

"Yes, that is right. It *does* get complicated, doesn't it?" Simeon mused. "But now, do you understand how the laws of cause and effect caused the events between Gwendolyn and Jeanne-Louise to come about?" Simeon asked Thomas.

"Yes, Sir." Thomas said. "I think I see the bigger picture much more clearly, though it is hard to believe that Sunitia's and my morals would decline that much, even amidst the dark influence of Kali Yuga.

"And I am so very sorry for what I did! What is to be done to expiate all the useless suffering caused by me (and by her, also), which I can imagine has repeated itself through many lifetimes?"

"We sometimes call it 'flip-flop karma,'" Simeon said. "Do you understand what is meant by that term?"

"All too well," Thomas sighed and then said, out loud and very vigorously. "Is it over, Sir, this 'flip-flop' and terrible karmic pattern between Sunitia and myself? I want to be done with it! Please show me what to do if it isn't over!"

"Be peaceful, my son. That particular pattern of karma is long finished between the two of you. Would you like to know how that happened?"

"Yes, very much so! Thank you, Sir. I am very grateful for any help you can give me in understanding more completely what happened between us!

"But first I must ask this one question: Was Sunitia really Jesus's cousin? Did she follow him in that lifetime as Miriam, listen to his teachings, and yet still have such violent thoughts of revenge at the time of her death? How is that possible?"

"Not everyone who is a follower of one of the Great Ones, such as Jesus, is able to fully absorb and act upon their teachings. Sunitia's time spent with Jesus was very important for her as a soul, and it did have a powerful impact on many of her future lives. But her contact with him in that lifetime wasn't enough to overcome her feelings about her death by a vicious murderer — after all, she was sure that what had happened to her was completely unfair. What had she done to deserve such a sudden and terrible death?

"Miriam, in that lifetime, had descended quite a bit from her highly evolved consciousness as Sunitia. Such a descent can happen, you know — remember our previous discussions about this subject? A soul can lose ground and fall backwards very far, perhaps even enough to need *temporarily* to inhabit an animal's body! Sunitia's regression wasn't so extreme, but still, in that lifetime, she was unable to understand why Jesus had taught that we must love and forgive each other always.

"And why did Jesus teach such forgiveness and love? Because all of us need to forgive each other for past actions. In our essential nature we are all perfect, and we are all one with one another. To hate another or wish him or her harm is *really* to hate and harm ourselves.

113

"These are very subtle teachings! Most of those who heard Jesus teach about forgiveness didn't really grasp the 'why' behind it. He often said about his teachings: 'For those who have ears to hear, let them hear.' He knew that many of his followers couldn't yet understand all of his words fully."

Simeon continued: "Do you have more questions about this matter just now?"

"No, Sir. I think I'm ready to see how and when Sunitia and I broke through this karmic pattern. Except that. . . ."

Simeon smiled: "Let me guess. You are hoping you don't have to be a woman again in your next time-travel adventure?"

This time Thomas laughed out loud, "Well, perhaps there's a small portion of that wish in my mind — though I *do* feel that I'm getting more comfortable with being in either a male or a female body. But primarily I was hoping to move away from Kali Yuga into a more enlightened yuga for my next time-travel experience. The dreariness and unreasonable violence of that dark age is starting to get to me!"

"It is good that you are feeling more comfortable in roles that change between male or female depending on the lifetime. And the lifetime which you will observe next is in the most recent Ascending Dwapara Yuga — we don't need to return to Kali Yuga any time soon, if you prefer."

Relieved at this news, Thomas quickly thought of another question, "If I understand you correctly, you are saying that this trip will take me to a time when Sunitia and I have stopped killing each other and become friends again? Or lovers?" Thomas couldn't keep the hopeful note out of his thoughts.

Simeon laughed, "You don't give up easily, do you, Thomas? But to answer your question, yes, you did resolve this karmic pattern nicely, but perhaps not in the way you are visualizing. Best we simply go there and observe, don't you think?"

"Yes, I'm ready and eager! When and where are we going?" Thomas enthused.

"Quite an interesting era, I think. It took place in a year the people of that time called 1947 AD (or 247 Ascending Dwapara Yuga, as we call it now). The place is California in the United States of America — a strong nation in its time, but long since dissolved. Your name was Jaydon and you were having an important and life-changing dream. This visit won't take very long. Would you like to observe your dream now?" Simeon asked.

"Yes! Experiencing an important dream in a past life should be fascinating. I'm ready to go wherever and whenever you want to guide me."

Thomas was getting much better at the mechanics of time travel; he quickly readied himself for the "journey."

CHAPTER 27

Jaydon was asleep and dreaming about his dearest friend. In the dream he realized that this beloved friend had turned against him in a drastic and harsh way. This dear friend was someone he had deeply trusted. The betrayal was agonizing — he felt the pain to the core of his being. In the dream, he felt the stinging pain of dark betrayal, and he also felt a desire for revenge — he wanted to cause his friend to feel the same pain he was feeling.

Finally, in the dream, which had "fast-forwarded" to the last moments of his life, he reflected carefully that if he left this world with the thought of revenge foremost in his mind, he would have to reincarnate in a situation that allowed him to betray his friend and give him the same sort of piercing pain he had felt even to his dying day.

His vision enlarged to see many lifetimes stretching out before him: one life in which he had his revenge against his friend for his betrayal, followed by another life in which his friend retaliated by betraying him once more; then, another life in which he once again succumbed to the desire to retaliate the wrong that had been done to him.

On and on it went from a distant past into an indefinite future, following a similar back-and-forth pattern of betrayal and revenge. Jaydon, in the midst of his "deathbed dream," suddenly realized that he could stop this cycle.

With all of his will power, strength, and energy, he cried out, "I forgive you! I *forgive*!"

The words and thoughts were put forth with such energy that he felt a huge bolt of power emerge from his being, freeing him from the karmic pattern between himself and his friend, then and there, forever. If his friend had a wish to cause further pain or betrayal to anyone, it would have to be to someone else. For him, what had seemed might become an endless cycle of revenge was finished. The trail of 'flip-flop karma' was over! What incredible freedom he felt. What joy!

Instantly awakened from his dream, Jaydon/Thomas knew that this was more than just a dream. He knew that through the strong act of forgiveness in his dream, he had been freed from future lifetimes of revenge-filled karma and personal suffering. He was very grateful. He felt light and free.

Thomas was soon back with Simeon. He was amazed at this shortest and most profound segment of time travel. Before he could transmit a single thought or question, Simeon began sending him soothing waves of love, telling him to be still and silent for a little while.

Finally Simeon said softly, "You do realize who 'the friend' was in Jaydon's dream, don't you?"

"Yes, I do! And I think I understand now the immense power of true forgiveness. But did Sunitia subsequently forgive me also — with equal force and determination not to continue in that betrayal/revenge pattern with me or anyone else?"

"Yes, fortunately it is true. And now it is time to meditate deeply on what you have learned from this experience." That was all that Simeon would communicate — their time together was at an end for today. It was time to refresh, recharge, and get ready for whatever was coming next.

CHAPTER 28

The weeks flew by. Some of the time Thomas spent with Simeon and his classmates, enjoying lively discussions and comparing notes about the many lessons this intense period of time travel was teaching them.

Thomas was dutifully recording each new sequence of time travel, as Simeon had asked him to do. The volume of information was growing to huge proportions. Thomas found he had a flair for describing, in great detail, all that he observed along the way. He enjoyed this part of the process almost as much as a time-travel experience itself.

But most of the time, he was still making journeys, moving rapidly though many time frames, learning more about his previous lives and understanding past yugas more deeply.

The deep emotional attachment to being with Sunitia never fully left Thomas — but he did feel that he had moved into a more peaceful state of mind about the whole matter. He never spoke of it with his classmates, and very seldom, anymore, even with Simeon. He knew better than to beg and plead, as he had once done, to be reunited with his lost love.

None of his classmates, in telling experiences of their own time travels, ever spoke of meeting such a "soul mate." Perhaps, he thought, they had had similar experiences, and they too guarded this information as too personal to discuss. Only with Sabella, that one time, had he unburdened his heart and, of course, many times, early in the process when he was so troubled, with Simeon.

One fine spring day — it always seemed like a glorious spring day in this part of Ascending Treta Yuga — Simeon asked Thomas to stay after class for a conference.

"Thomas, I have looked through the chronicle you are keeping. It is excellently composed, and I want to compliment you on how well you're capturing the flavor and essence of the many lives and places you are visiting."

Thomas tried hard to remain humble — praise like this from Simeon was rare. Love and gratitude for his teacher once again swelled in his heart.

"Thank you, Sir. I've tried hard to be truthful and accurate, and to record the feelings I have had in all of these wildly different times and places. I know that your guidance has been invaluable."

Simeon went on to make a request. "Please create a list of your time-travel experiences so far, in the order in which you have re-lived them now. Also include a brief summary of what you saw or learned in each one — two or three sentences is plenty."

"Two or three sentences to summarize a past lifetime?" Thomas laughed out loud — then became quickly sober when he saw that Simeon was serious.

Simeon went on: "I will help you whenever you feel bogged down in the 'condensation' process. There's an important reason for this exercise, so please begin as soon as possible."

"Yes, Sir, I will." Thomas smiled at Simeon as they both "watched" his mind race through the challenges and possible solutions to carrying out this assignment.

In his peaceful home that night, Thomas sat for meditation and prayed for guidance and divine help for his assignment. His four-hour meditation was helpful in removing most of his doubts, but afterwards he still felt slightly restless and confused. The night was beautiful and quiet. He decided that a walking meditation beside the nearby river was just what he needed right now.

The river rippled with a rustling AUM sound as he walked slowly beside the water. The reflection of the stars and a crescent moon danced on the river's surface. The smooth stones seemed to shine, each with its own inner light. He enjoyed the sweet fragrance of night-blooming flowers, wild herbs, and the rich soil in which they thrived. As he walked, he began to sing another ancient song that Simeon had taught him when he was very young. He was surprised that he remembered it so well — its simplicity and beauty were perfect for this moment. It was about the "devas," or nature spirits, who live all around us:

> You devas of woodland, of mountain and field:
>> Come shower on us blessings and light.
> The wonders that Nature, befriended, can yield
>> Reveal to our hearing and sight.
>>> Your melodies, whispering joy on the air,
>>> Affirm that God's ev'rywhere.
> O devas of woodland, of mountain and field,
>> Be with us in blessing this night.©

Thomas became so blissful and uplifted with all the inner and outer beauty he was experiencing, and with the presence of God within and all around him, that he simply had to sit down and go completely within himself in meditation. Many hours later, he came back to conscious awareness. It was full daylight and he was sitting on a boulder by the sun-drenched river.

To his great surprise, Sabella was sitting on a boulder nearby, apparently in deep meditation. Not wanting to disturb her, he began to move away as quietly as possible. Not quietly enough though, for he heard her speak his name mentally.

"Thomas, please don't go yet. There is something I need to say to you."

Thomas didn't want to be with anyone at the moment, but he veiled this feeling and thought back to her, "Hello, Sabella. How may I help you?"

"Thomas, I was very troubled last night. I decided to do the walking meditation that Simeon has taught us, in hopes of re-centering myself. I chose this path along the river, thinking I'd be alone. Then I saw you sitting here — obviously deep in meditation. You seemed to be enveloped in a great bubble of golden and blue light. I was amazed and. . . ." Here she paused and ducked her head. "I'm sorry, Thomas, I couldn't resist partaking in a small part of what seemed to be happening for you. There was such bliss — such blessings — I couldn't leave — I just. . . ."

She stopped and looked into his eyes, vibrating a strong desire for his understanding and forgiveness at her intrusion in what was obviously a very private time.

"It is fine, Sabella. How long were you here with me?"

"I really don't know. Many hours — I think it's about noon now. Time stopped for me."

"And for me, also," Thomas said, and they both laughed delightedly.

Sabella stood up, walked over to Thomas and reached down to the ground near where he was standing to pick a stem of wild thyme. She gave it to him, and said: "No thyme like the present."

He smiled as he received her simple gift, "And now you and I both have thyme on our hands."

More laughter. "Thomas, I'll go now. I see you have much to contemplate. But thank you for letting me share this thyme/time with you. We'll talk more later if you like."

She walked away quietly. As she left, Thomas realized that he had not asked her what had been troubling her. But she was perfectly correct. He had many new ideas of his own to contemplate right now. He determined to see her later, to see how he might help her. He walked slowly home, through the fragrant meadows of flowers and wild thyme.

CHAPTER 29

At home, after a quick meal and a long shower of lightly scented and brightly-colored light (mint green was today's choice), he felt ready to begin listing his time-travel episodes, and giving a brief description of each.

Thomas was still not clear what the purpose of this exercise might be, since he had already carefully chronicled each journey in detail. Still, Simeon had been very definite in his request.

And so he began at the beginning.

1) First visit to Descending Treta Yuga in the year 4910 BC (1,810 years before the end of Descending Treta Yuga). Sunitia, my wife, and I. . . .

Here, he had to pause and think about what to say. What could be said? So much was packed into his first time-travel experience. He found that so many emotions were still stirred up in him when he began to contemplate it, that he decided to move on and come back to write about that one later.

2) Visit to Descending Kali Yuga in the year 160 BC (542 Descending Kali Yuga). My best friend, Caleb, and I fought in the Maccabbean Wars; we both died of our wounds.

3) The eleventh century in Normandy, 1070 AD (570 Ascending Kali Yuga). I was Gwendolyn, a servant of Queen Matilda, William the Conqueror's wife. I was poisoned — murdered by my daughter, Jeanne-Louise.

4) Descending Kali Yuga again, about 33 AD (733 Descending Kali Yuga). Abigail murdered her servant-girl Miriam.

5) Ascending Dwapara Yuga, 1800 AD (100 Ascending Dwapara Yuga). Strange experience in India digging up a yogi who had been buried under a lake (I was a worker, helping to drain the lake). When brought back to life, he asked, "What yuga is this?" On being told it was Kali Yuga (a mistake — it was early into Dwapara) he replied, "Then I'm not interested"

and immediately left his body. I never found out which yuga he was from, but Kali Yuga is definitely not a great place to be.

6) 700 BC (1 year into Descending Kali Yuga and the transition point from Descending Dwapara Yuga to Descending Kali Yuga). Fought as an archer beside the greatest of all warriors, Arjuna, in the Battle of Kurukshetra. Died early in the war, but felt privileged to have been with those super-heroes of the Mahabharata, especially Lord Krishna.

7) 1933 AD (233 Ascending Dwapara Yuga). A wonderful life as a woman disciple of Paramhansa Yogananda. Sunitia was there, too — a young monk, much younger than I. We had very little contact because our guru had asked the men and women monastic disciples not to mix with each other at all.

8) 2800 BC (302 years into Descending Dwapara Yuga). In Egypt, helping to manifest a great pharaoh's tomb, using both sweat and magic.

9) 600 BC (102 Descending Kali Yuga). Not happy to be in Kali Yuga again, but Greece was not a bad place to be at that time, on the whole. I met some wise philosophers, and thought I spotted Simeon among them. He wouldn't confirm this sighting when I returned.

10) 4099 AD (2399 Ascending Dwapara Yuga, at the transition between Ascending Dwapara and Ascending Treta Yugas). I was a woman and the president of the World Council, probably the most important person on Earth during a time of peace on the planet. I didn't stay long in that time frame, and didn't spot anybody I knew.

11) 4300 BC (in India again, in the time of Lord Rama, who lived in the second half of Descending Treta Yuga, about 2300 years after the beginning of Treta Yuga and about 1,300 years before the end of Descending Treta Yuga/beginning of Descending Dwapara). Rama was my king, but I never met him personally before he was exiled to the forest with his wife, Sita, and his faithful brother Lakshman. I did get to fight in the company of Hanuman, a sort of monkey-human, a great warrior, and primary disciple of Rama. Wonderful to meet such an unusual "person." Very uplifting.

12) 1968–2011 AD (268–311 Ascending Dwapara Yuga). Got to help found and live at Ananda Village in Northern California — an incredible place and the blueprint for similar communities that sprang up worldwide after the great "dark time." Sunitia was there too, but we were only friends. We did participate in many group meditations, which was great. In 2009 we both became members of the newly formed Nayaswami Monastic Order.

13) 5110 AD (1010 Ascending Dwapara Yuga). Eight hundred years before my present lifetime, I invented showers of scented, colored light (making water showers obsolete) and became extremely wealthy as a result of this invention. The money did not make me happy, but the fact that people enjoyed (and still do) taking scented, colored light showers makes me feel somewhat better about that lifetime now.

14) 2000 BC (1102 Descending Dwapara Yuga). Lived in China as a peasant. Not fun.

15) 1100 AD (600 Ascending Kali Yuga). Lived in North America as a Cherokee, a Native American. That *was* fun.

16) 8791 BC (2711 Descending Satya Yuga). Lived in Atlantis and experienced the continent's sinking into the ocean.

Thomas was growing tired of these recollections. Previously, he'd enjoyed writing up every little detail of a visit to a past life. There had been much to see and learn, though some lives had seemed more educational for various reasons. He realized he had had brief glimpses of the soul he called Sunitia in many, though not all, of his past lives.

After several hours of listing another forty or so episodes, he found his entries becoming shorter and shorter. He finally realized he couldn't stand any more recording. The past lives and yugas he had visited were beginning to blur together, and to take on a weird sameness. What had seemed exciting and interesting before didn't seem so anymore.

He then remembered that Simeon had hinted to all his students that they would eventually get tired of visiting past lives and past yugas. Even if he reached one hundred past-life visits (his unofficial goal when he began his time-travel adventures), he was beginning to realize that he'd still have revisited only a tiny fraction of the millions, or perhaps billions, of lives he had already lived — this now was a truly daunting thought. A sense of anguishing monotony began to cloud his anticipation of further time travel.

It was definitely time to quit and do something else. He decided to visit Sabella.

He didn't contact her ahead of time to ask if he could pay a visit, an omission which was probably thoughtless of him. But in his mind he kept remembering her troubled demeanor at the river, and he felt compelled to see what was going on with her.

Sabella was at home. She was surprised to see Thomas show up without any notice. It was not like him to be impolite in this way.

"Sabella, forgive me. I was unable to continue working on the most recent assignment Simeon has given me, so I decided to come see you — sorry I didn't take time to pre-announce myself. I was wondering if I could be of any help to you. You mentioned that you were troubled before you came to that spot along the river. Is there something you would feel comfortable discussing with me — maybe it would help?"

Sabella was touched by her friend's concern. She decided that it might be a good idea to share what had been bothering her.

"Thomas, I don't know where you are in your time-travel experiences. I mean, how many visits have you made to past lives — do you mind if I ask that question?"

"No, not at all. My most recent time-travel event brought my total to eighty-nine trips in all — I established a goal for myself, with Simeon's approval, of a hundred visits to the past. At that point we were going to stop and see if I wanted or needed to continue in this process."

Sabella smiled, "You are a bit ahead of me. I didn't set a specific goal, but I've had only sixty-eight experiences."

"Is that what's troubling you?" Thomas asked. "The numbers don't really matter, you know. We've both been time traveling extensively for over three years now and perhaps you stayed longer in some of the times and places you visited than I did."

"Perhaps, but that is not my concern at the moment. It's more that I'm getting the feeling that I don't want to continue with this process much longer. Simeon had me recording each visit in detail, which I have faithfully done so far. Now he has asked me to compile a simple list of sorts, just recording the visit, time, place, and a phrase or so about what happened there."

Thomas was very interested to hear this! "He asked me to do that exact thing, Sabella, the last time we met together. How is it going for you?"

"That is what is weighing on my mind. I've completed my list. I've begun to see many of the same patterns weaving themselves together through these past-life experiences. I think this may be what Simeon wants us to see as part of the exercise.

"For example, it did not matter whether I was a man or a woman, rich or poor, smart or stupid; I had many different occupations in all these different times and places — still there was an essential *me* there, doing whatever was to be done in my own unique way.

"I know Simeon has told us often that no matter what happens to us, through our many lives, we always remain, in a certain way, ourselves. I loved the way he put it: 'Sabella, you have a unique song to sing in this universe. No one else can sing that song in the same way as you. So whether you sing it well or not, it is still going to be yours alone, and unlike anyone else's. You are specializing on behalf of the whole universe in being a Sabella-pirate or a Sabella-king or a Sabella-beggar, and no one else can do that in quite the same way.'

"He had told us that before, and finally I began to see it for myself, firsthand. That part was very enlightening! But still, as I compiled the list, I began to become tired of the review. I realized that re-living sixty-eight of my past lives is a 'drop in the bucket' among all the lives I've lived. It's beginning to seem like this might be an exercise in futility. No matter what I do, I'm always going to be some version of me. I think I want to stop time traveling."

At this she lowered her head and turned away from Thomas, thinking perhaps she had said too much.

"Sabella, that is *exactly* what I have been thinking while making a similar list of my time-travel experiences. I had thought that a hundred past-life visits would simply whet my appetite for hundreds, maybe thousands more visits to the past. Instead, trying to compile my list has done just the opposite. I was not yet ready to say, 'Enough of this!' — I had not yet crystallized that thought as well as you seem to have done. But now that I hear you say this, I'm sure that I feel exactly the same way! I think I may want to stop time traveling altogether!"

Sabella looked up at him with relief on her face. "You do? I'm so glad you have told me how you feel. It will give me cour-age to tell Simeon what I'm feeling also, though he probably already knows all about it."

"Yes, that's true." They exchanged a few more thoughts on the subject. When Thomas left her home, he found that he felt much better; he now felt ready to consult Simeon about what he and Sabella had discussed — that perhaps it was time for him to stop visiting his past lives.

CHAPTER 30

The next day Thomas went to clarify his feelings with Simeon. Before he could think a single word, Simeon sent him this thought: "I believe it is time to move into a slightly different phase of your time-travel adventures. It's time to take a look at the future."

Thomas was taken aback and at the same time thrilled. All thoughts of terminating his time-travel experiences vanished. He knew that the honor of traveling into the future was not bestowed on every time-travel student. In fact, none of his classmates had yet done so; no one had even mentioned the possibility. Simeon had discussed future travel to the class only very briefly, but said that they wouldn't be traveling forward in time any time soon, if ever.

Thomas wondered, "Are we talking about the future in general, or *my* future?"

Simeon was quick to pick up Thomas's thoughts, as always. He answered, "For you, I believe a more personal look may be best. For traveling into the future we use a slightly different method, which I will explain to you soon. Instead of re-living a future life, which you couldn't do since you have not lived through any future life yet. . . ."

Here Simeon paused and then added, ". . . well, actually, in a certain sense this is not completely true. As we have discussed before, time is a delusion. The past, present, and future all exist (and don't exist) simultaneously. But travel forward, as far as our regular senses are concerned, is best done in a certain way, in order not to influence what happens in your future. You will have a very short glimpse, because knowing too much about the future might have an adverse effect on your present life."

"I may not be able to change the past, but I can certainly change the future, because it hasn't happened yet!" They both chuckled at this familiar time-travel maxim.

Simeon continued, "Of course, there is also always the hope that you don't have to have any future lives, or at least very few of them — that through the deepening of your meditations, you will achieve final liberation, freedom from the seemingly endless wheel of karma and reincarnation."

Thomas realized that, in mentioning Thomas's traveling to a future lifetime, Simeon was saying that he did, indeed, have a future life (or lives) to live. He wasn't sure how to feel about *this* idea. He was a little disappointed, now that he thought about it. Ah well. . . .

Simeon smiled: "Thomas, it is not for me to tell you how many more lifetimes you have to live. But if you apply yourself to continued deep meditation, they will be very few by comparison to those countless lives you have already lived."

"Countless!" Thomas was so startled, he spoke out loud. "What do you mean, 'countless'?"

"Don't fret, my son. I was using that word just to indicate a very large number."

"How many, Sir? How long have I been doing this? How much longer does it have to go on for me?" Thomas was beginning to feel desperate.

"I have told you before that I will *not* answer these questions for you, Thomas, but I *can* remind you that you will know the answer to these questions (and all questions) when you achieve final liberation and oneness with God. However, at that point, the exact number of past lives you've lived will not matter to you at all. You will merge back into the great Ocean of Blissful Spirit, from whence you came."

Simeon continued. "When you or any student ask *when* final liberation will happen, how do you think I would answer that question?"

"Enigmatically, no doubt; evasively, probably."

Simeon raised an eyebrow.

"I know, I know," Thomas went on somewhat peevishly. "We have free will to a certain extent. And relative to all the lives we've lived — we are almost free. And to the degree that we apply ourselves to meditation and right attitudes — well, our earnest self-effort and the grace of God will determine the 'when' of it all."

"Yes," said Simeon and changed the subject.

"It can sometimes be beneficial to get a glimpse of a higher age than the one you live in right now. We might do this by going backward and seeing a Satya Yuga of the past, but for you, Thomas, for various reasons, which I think you'll understand better soon, we are going to try a 'forward jump' into the higher age of Ascending Satya Yuga that this planet will begin to move into 1,790 years from now."

Satya Yuga! What an amazing era to contemplate. Even though the world around Thomas and Simeon, in the present time of Ascending Treta Yuga, was very advanced in many ways, there were many aspects of life in Satya Yuga that were more subtle, different, and difficult to comprehend by people in *any* of the lower yugas.

For example, Thomas had learned that in Satya Yuga, war, or even a threat of hostility, will no longer exist. Harmony will reign in the hearts of all creatures. People and nature will live together in complete fearlessness and joy. Animals will be easily able to communicate with one another and with humans. Flying through the air will be a commonplace form of recreation, while instant teleportation will be the main mode of transportation.

In Satya Yuga, the veils between the different universes — physical, astral, and causal — will be very thin. The angels, saints, masters, gods, and goddesses will interact with human beings on a regular basis. Nature will be completely benevolent and cooperative in every way.

The climate will be ideal and few people will bother to live in a house — though they could materialize any structure they desired. Why would anyone want a house when one could live safely, harmoniously, and in perfect comfort among the beauties of nature?

No one will ever be hungry — in fact, eating food as we do now will not be necessary. Light rays will be absorbed as needed and converted into life force. Illness and disease will be nonexistent. Injuries will happen rarely, and any injury would be able to be healed instantly.

"Heaven on earth! Almost incomprehensible in its perfection," thought Thomas, as he now reflected on what he had learned about Satya Yuga.

"Well, not quite, but close," answered Simeon. "Certainly much better than any yuga you've experienced in your recent time travels."

"When I get there, will I want not to return here?" Thomas queried.

"Possibly, but that won't be an option, as you'll see."

Simeon now began to coach Thomas on the technique of how to travel forward in time. Thomas was cautioned never to share this technique without Simeon's permission and *never* to try it without supervision.

Simeon then transported Thomas and himself to a place Thomas had never been, nor had even suspected existed.

"What is this place, Sir?" he asked as he looked around in awe.

"This is the Chapel of Future Light."

Indeed, the "building" seemed not to be made of matter, but of light. They were now inside a sphere of swirling light. As Thomas looked around more closely, he could see that the light was filled with shapes and colors, scenes of places he didn't know, and objects he couldn't identify. He tried to focus his eyes on a particular pattern, but it changed too quickly to show exactly what it was. He sensed that there were beings of light present, but the light patterns were moving too quickly for him to see more than that.

"Sit down, Thomas," Simeon said.

"Where, Sir?" Thomas asked. He felt himself floating inside

the spherical chapel and could see no surfaces upon which to sit.

"Right where you are."

Thomas did as his teacher suggested, folded his legs in the Lotus Pose, and "sat." At once he felt comfortably supported; but when he looked to see what was supporting him, there seemed to be only more swirling lights and colors.

Simeon "sat" facing his student and said, "Thomas, we'll begin the 'future-travel' technique as I have taught you. But there is one thing I have not yet revealed to you.

"I will be going with you into the future." Simeon shared this news solemnly with his eager student.

This was quite a surprise! One of the primary "rules" of time travel, or at least Thomas had thought it a primary rule, was that you always went alone. It was *your* life that you were re-visiting, no one else's. Although you could talk about it and chronicle it when you returned, during the journey itself, it was a very personal experience.

Thomas simply couldn't resist asking, "Why, Sir? Will I need help?"

Simeon only smiled and said, "You will understand soon."

CHAPTER 31

⌒𝓂⌒

"Diligently following one's chosen path,
and cleansing oneself thereby of all karmic debts
the yogi, after many births, attains perfection
and enters at last into the Supreme Beatitude."

— Bhagavad Gita 6:45

Thomas and Simeon were invisibly floating above planet Earth. Simeon had told him before they departed that they would be visiting the year 7750 AD (50 Ascending Satya Yuga), about 1,840 years in their future.

"Planet Earth is a completely beautiful and perfect place now, isn't it Thomas?"

"Yes, Sir, it does look that way. I've seen other inhabited planets and I know there are millions more that I have not seen, but this Earth is still very lovely and somehow still feels like home. I'm amazed that it doesn't look that different for being over 1,800 years into our future, at least from this distance."

"Look more closely," Simeon hinted.

He did as Simeon instructed and saw that the shapes of the continents as he knew them were different. There were still oceans, but the land had shifted about a bit.

"Yes, Sir, I see some differences now."

"What else do you notice, Thomas?"

"The clouds! Where are the clouds?"

"No need for them in Satya Yuga. Remember, the climate is perfect. Any water that is needed for plant life forms at night as a sort of mist or dew. Let's move closer."

They "landed" on a beach, unlike any Thomas had ever seen or imagined. Each grain of sand was a tiny diamond. Thomas scooped up some of the sand in his hand and said somewhat foolishly, "These look like diamonds."

"As well they might, Thomas, because they are."

Thomas continued to look around. This was obviously an ocean, for there were large waves rolling up on to the diamond beach. The water seemed perfectly clear and was a brilliant turquoise color. But something was missing — what was it? The smell! Thomas couldn't detect that salty smell that a beach always has.

"Taste the water, Thomas," Simeon said. He did and found to his great surprise that the water was not salty! In fact, it was more delicious than any water Thomas had ever tasted. An ocean of clean, clear water that tasted like sweet nectar! He was tempted to wade further into it and drink more and more, but he resisted. He felt that Simeon would rather they didn't tarry here.

"What now, Sir?"

"Let's take a brief tour of this part of planet Earth in Satya Yuga."

And so they flew about, delighting in the radiant beauty everywhere. There were no dead or diseased plants or animals, no barren deserts or icy wildernesses. All was a garden of unsurpassed beauty. There were not very many people to be seen. Those who were visible seemed to be occupied in meditation, either alone or in small groups. Others were communing with plants and animals in ways that Thomas couldn't understand.

There were artists, musicians, sculptors, and architects who seemed to be working harmoniously to create beautiful edifices made of light and sound. Much of what Thomas saw he couldn't put into words. It was not in his range of past experiences and therefore incomprehensible to him.

Still, he knew beauty when he saw it, and he felt vibrations of peace and joy everywhere. Everyone seemed very happy and peaceful. He wanted to linger in each locale they saw, but Simeon moved them along fairly rapidly.

After some time, Simeon directed them to a small hillside covered with brilliant violet flowers. The flowers smelled exceedingly sweet and seemed to be singing. Thomas was entranced as they sat in the soft mellow light and listened to "flower music." A butterfly with flashing rainbow wings flew about his head, and when he reached out his hand in wonder, the butterfly lit on his hand, turned her golden eyes in Thomas's direction and clearly transmitted these words: "Follow me, follow me!"

Simeon smiled at Thomas's delight. When the butterfly flew away, they followed her, up and around the flowered slope to a small cave opening. The butterfly flew inside and vanished from their sight.

Simeon said to Thomas, "Go inside, my son. There is no danger here. I will wait here for you to return. This part is for you to experience alone."

Thomas moved slowly and reverently into the small cave — deep vibrations of holiness and peace emanated from the opening. A little stream flowed through the cave, making tiny pools of liquid light. The walls seemed to glow from within, creating a soft light all around him. When Thomas touched a wall, it felt warm and alive; it seemed to vibrate slightly.

The cave seemed to radiate comfort and welcome. It also felt oddly familiar, though Thomas couldn't imagine how that could be. After all, he was in the future now! Strolling along for a few more minutes, he came to a "room" in the cave.

Seated at the far wall, just beside a pool of water, he saw a person sitting. He instantly knew that he was seeing himself — his future self. And even as he had that thought, he also knew that this person was . . . different, somehow not the same "self" that he thought he knew — words and thoughts failed him.

"What should I do now?" he wondered.

"Just relax and observe," came the answer inside his head. Thomas didn't know where the answer had come from. It hadn't come from Simeon, but it sounded very familiar.

Thomas didn't go closer to the seated figure. He didn't want to disturb the person's obviously deep meditation. He sat down and watched and waited. Soon he felt drawn into deep meditation, himself.

A vision came softly, with no fanfare. He saw the person (himself?) sitting motionless in the cave room, by the small pool. He noticed that the person's form was reflected in the glass-like pool, but that it wasn't a mirror image of the person. It was somebody else! How strange! Now, in the vision, he saw the two forms begin slowly to merge into each other. Finally there was a flash of brilliant light and they were both gone. He was filled with indescribable joy at this sight. He returned to an even deeper, thought-free meditation.

"Thomas!" This time it *was* Simeon's voice, sounding very far away.

"I am here," said Thomas, though he was not sure what, where, or when "here" was.

Coming back to awareness, Thomas found himself back in the Chapel of Future Light, floating beside Simeon.

Simeon said, "Thomas, we will leave the Chapel now and go to my home for a time of reflection on what you have seen and experienced of your future in Satya Yuga."

CHAPTER 32

Thomas felt blissfully above and beyond his normal state of consciousness. At the same time, he felt dazed and confused.

Simeon sliced some ripe fruit and they ate slowly together in silence.

Finally, Thomas couldn't contain himself. "Simeon, Sir, . . . what was it I witnessed in the cave? Was it a vision? Was it real? Was that person me? Who was the person reflected in the water of the pool?"

"Thomas, I could read your mind now and find out the details of what you remember, but I think it would be better for you to relive it by telling me exactly what you remember. If you still don't understand what you saw, I'll help you."

Thomas went over the details as he remembered them. As he retold it all in as much detail as possible, he began to understand the meaning of what he had seen.

"Sir, I believe I saw the moment in my future when I achieved *samadhi* — oneness with God. Could that be possible?"

"Yes," was Simeon's simple reply.

"But who was the other person reflected in the water? Why did the two of them merge into one being?" Even as he asked the question he knew the answer. "It was the other half of my soul, wasn't it? It was. . . ." Here he stopped. He was going to say Sunitia's name, but suddenly, all her/his other names and faces flashed before his consciousness and all his own names and past lives were there in his mind also.

"Who am I?" he cried. "Who is she? We are one! We are all one." Instant understanding flooded his heart and mind. It was a revelation beyond imagination of expectancy.

He fell at Simeon's feet and wept with joy. Simeon only smiled and sent blessings to his dear student.

"Get up, Thomas!" Simeon cried. "We need to walk by the river and watch the sunset on this glorious day."

CHAPTER 33

Thomas went to his home and didn't leave it for a month or so. He did this at Simeon's request and because he very much wanted solitude and reflection — more than ever before in this lifetime.

But just before he began his time of seclusion in earnest, he had an important conversation with Simeon.

"Sir, before we viewed my future lifetime in Ascending Satya Yuga, I had come to tell you that I didn't think I wanted to do any more traveling through past lives and past yugas. I think I've seen enough to understand what I needed to learn from the process. Am I correct in that thought?"

"Yes, you are right. You had a good 'run,' but I can see that you have become tired of it — for all the right reasons. You have begun to see the patterns and the anguishing monotony of life after life. There is no need now for you to experience more of them.

"I think you realize that the memories of all these lives reside within your subconscious mind and your Higher Self. Although they are unique to you as a soul, they do not all have to be re-lived or remembered in order to teach you the lessons you learned while living them. You now have the 'golden key' that opens all doors to all your past lives. I doubt you'll need to use it again — still, it is yours now and forever."

"Sir, I intuitively know that I have the 'key' as you say, but please explain to me more fully what that key is and how, exactly, I got it."

"Thomas, we *did* study this, but I'll remind you once again. Remember Patanjali, the very ancient teacher who lived in Descending Kali Yuga?"

"Yes, Sir, I remember Patanjali. He was the great exponent and preserver of the yoga sciences, especially through his eightfold path to liberation. His Yoga Sutras miraculously remained valid and clear through the darkest parts of Kali Yuga and were brought to light and clarified again in Ascending Dwapara Yuga."

Simeon continued, "I'll remind you now of the explanation by Sri Nayaswami Kriyananda (who lived and taught in early Ascending Dwapara Yuga) of the last of the *yamas*, the first 'limb' of Patanjali's eightfold path:"

> The last of the five *yamas* (virtues) is called *Aparigraha* in Sanskrit. It means non-greed or non-attachment.
>
> Non-greed has often been translated to mean the non-receiving of gifts. I read Patanjali's meaning differently. He says, later on, that when a person becomes perfected in this virtue he can remember his former incarnations. What has the non-receiving of gifts to do with such a memory? Patanjali is not even talking of specific practices, but rather of states of consciousness. Non-greed is closer to the right translation. It differs from Patanjali's third rule of non-covetousness in the sense that non-covetousness means not to desire what is not rightfully one's own, while non-greed means not to be attached even to what already *is* one's own. Non-greed, perfectly practiced, leads one to become non-attached even to his own body. It is by such perfect non-attachment that the blindness of temporary identifications is overcome, with the result that one can remember his past identifications with other bodies, other places and events.
>
> The yogi should realize that everything is God. Greed, or attachment, limits the mind to one body, and obscures the truth that the soul is, in essence, infinite and eternal.

---

*Swami Kriyananda (J. Donald Walters) *The Art and Science of Raja Yoga*, Step Four—I. Philosophy (Nevada City, CA: Crystal Clarity Publishers, 2002, Hansa Trust).

Paramhansa Yogananda once said to a disciple: "You have a sour taste in your mouth, haven't you?"

"How could you know?" asked the surprised disciple.

"Because," replied the Master, "I am just as much in your body as I am in my own."

Freedom from physical limitations is no imaginary state, though even as such it would be preferable to imaginary bondage. But it can only be achieved if one is so perfectly non-attached to his limitations that they are no longer limiting to him.

In meditation, you will find it helpful to free yourself mentally from all worldly identifications. Cut the emotional strings that tie you to your possessions. Completely relax your body. Affirm mentally: *"I am not the body! I am Spirit — ever blissful — ever free!"**

Simeon and Thomas paused for a while to absorb these powerful words. Then Simeon asked, "Do you fully understand now what the key is — that key that will let you know about all your past incarnations?"

Thomas replied enthusiastically, "Thank you, Sir. I think I can communicate it more clearly now. Through deeper and longer meditations, I am becoming less and less attached to everything, even to my own body. The blindness of temporary identifications with any of my lifetimes, and even with the body I inhabit right now, is leaving me.

"The result of this level of non-attachment is that I can remember *all* my past identifications with other bodies, other places, and events, and know that none of them can bind me to delusion. I've begun to realize that everything is part of a great Ocean of Awareness — there is no separation between lifetimes or anything or anyone! This is surely the key of which you speak."

"Not only I!" Simeon said. "But all those who have lived before us and have realized these truths — all of us are moving ever upward, along that same pathway to final liberation."

Thomas said, "One final question for today, please. Why did you need to go with me into the future?"

"I wanted to be sure that the shock of witnessing that first moment of omnipresence did not render you unable to return to the here and now."

Thomas recalled that he didn't remember anything for a while (he had no idea how long) after the blinding flash of light he saw in the cave.

"I think I understand," Thomas reflected softly. "You shepherded me back here. Thank you — I guess." They both smiled in understanding.

"Yes, Thomas. You needed to come back to this time and place again, even though I knew how much your soul longed to stay there. There are still many things for you to learn here in Ascending Treta Yuga."

CHAPTER 34

The month of seclusion passed very quickly. Thomas used most of his time to go deeper and deeper into meditation.

When Thomas finally returned to the Halls of Wisdom to join his classmates and Simeon, he felt very strong and filled with joyful anticipation to learn what else might be in store for all of them.

He was surprised when Sabella met him at the gateway and asked to speak to him privately before they joined the others.

"Thomas, I don't know how to tell you this, but . . . I guess I'll just say it: Simeon is gone."

"Gone? Gone where?"

"We don't know. We've looked in his home and other places we thought he might be, but he has disappeared completely. Do you have any idea what might have happened to him?"

"Perhaps he is visiting the 'higher realms.' He once spoke of them to me very briefly. He said, 'I don't live my life completely alone as many of you think. I, too, have my mentors and instructors. There are those more spiritually advanced than I, with whom I consult as needed.'"

Sabella brightened. "Good idea. Let's go inside and tell the others!"

They did this, but unfortunately no one, including Thomas, had the slightest idea where the "higher realms" might be or how one might contact Simeon there, if he were indeed in that unknown place. And why would he leave without saying a word to anyone?

As they exchanged thoughts and ideas, they noticed that, unusually, *everyone* was there. For most of the last three years, at any one given time, at least half of their classmates were away on time-travel adventures.

Vilma voiced this realization aloud with great astonishment:

"Think of it! We're all here together today! Simeon must have engineered this gathering. What could it possibly mean?"

After a bit more discussion and brainstorming, Loralon surprised everyone with this idea: "Let's meditate together for a long time, with the common purpose of contacting Simeon wherever he may be."

Vilma said with a quavering voice, "Loralon, are you saying Simeon could be dead?" She could not stop the tears that appeared in her eyes.

It was a thought that no one had yet been willing even to entertain. The bonds of love with their revered teacher were very strong.

Thomas now sent this thought: "Friends, I do not sense that Simeon has left the material plane. I think we would feel it inside if he had, don't you?"

Several students nodded in agreement.

He continued: "Loralon is right. Thank you, Loralon, for your excellent suggestion. I agree that we should have a group meditation, for a much longer time than usual — shall we say all day tomorrow, if Simeon has not returned or contacted us by then? Between now and then, we will pray for guidance. Perhaps Simeon or someone from this 'higher realm' will appear to us, to explain what is going on."

145

CHAPTER 35

The following day, they gathered together under a giant shade tree — a beautiful, quiet place where they had meditated together many times. Thomas was told that his fellow students had appointed him to lead the group meditation. They had decided on a twelve-hour period of concentrated group meditation. He led a brief prayer for guidance, reminding them to begin their meditation by setting aside all desires, even the great, mutual desire to find Simeon.

"Use your techniques of Kriya Yoga for the first six hours of our meditation. Go deep into the silence. At the end of that first period of meditation, we'll chant together, to unite our hearts in God. In the second half, after a bit more silent-mind, open-heart time, and when we are as united superconsciously as possible, I'll try to guide us in seeking Simeon inwardly, in whatever ways may seem best at that time. Stay open and uplifted; surely we'll find the answers we need. Blessings to us all now. Go deep!"

After about nine hours of meditation, nothing had happened. They had called inwardly and deeply on the power of God and the forces of the universe. Refusing to be discouraged, Thomas asked Sabella, whose voice was very sweet, to lead them in a chant.

"Let's chant together for an hour; is that alright with everybody?" Sabella said. Agreement came.

And so with one mind and one heart, they sang for an hour these simple words to a beautiful, old melody:

Reveal Thyself, Reveal Thyself, Reveal Thyself,
Reveal Thyself!©

The words were addressed primarily, as they had been taught from childhood, to God and their own higher Selves. But now, of course, there was also the hint of asking Simeon to reveal himself.

Fifty minutes into the chanting, they continued singing not aloud, but silently in their hearts. They realized that they were no longer chanting the chant, the chant was chanting them! This was the "superconscious chanting" of which the Great Ones often spoke. It was thrilling for all of them to experience.

Sabella had also stopped singing, but continued to play the chant very softly on her musical instrument. Now she played more and more softly until even that very soft music died away into silence.

In the silence, a soft and familiar voice came into their minds: "I am here. Beautiful music, my children. Surpassingly beautiful chanting! My heart is melted with joy!"

Eyes flew open at once and there he was, standing beside the big tree, his hand resting on its giant trunk.

"Simeon!" They said as one voice. Some of them started to rise and to move toward him.

"Please stay where you are. I will greet each of you individually later. I'm sorry to have caused you concern about my whereabouts. I know you are wondering where I have been and why I gave you no notice about my disappearance. Thomas was right. I have been with the Higher Council for a few days. It has been decided that I join their ranks now."

There was silence and shock among the students as they digested this news.

"Where, exactly, will you be, Sir?" Sabella asked on behalf of all of them.

"That is something you will know when it is time for you to know. I cannot invite you to visit me there, but I will come back often to see you, for I love you all very much! Please understand that this is the culmination of many years of service to you and to many others. It is time for me to serve in a different way now."

"But what shall we do for a teacher? Who will guide and protect us? Are we to discontinue our time-travel experiments?"

Many questions barraged Simeon.

He smiled and held his hands up in a familiar gesture of "Peace, please!"

"As I have said, I will be back many times for visits. A few of you have completed your personal time-travel experiences." Here he glanced meaningfully at Sabella and Thomas. "Others of you should continue for a while."

Simeon continued: "I am now appointing two from among you, Thomas and Sabella, to carry on in my place as your primary instructors and guides, and I will guide them. Through them, I will still be with you."

More shocked silence as all eyes turned on Thomas and Sabella. They both kept their eyes fixed on Simeon's face, feeling great power pouring through him into their beings. Both were speechless and without thought, feeling deep bliss and the rightness of the decision.

"Sabella, Thomas, please come forward to me now for my blessing."

They did so without hesitation, touching his feet and kneeling before him for a few moments. He reached down to indicate that they should stand up facing him. His touch was light as a feather, and it filled them with energy and inspiration.

"Dear ones, I will speak to both of you privately about your new leadership roles, but for now, I want to offer you all my blessings for your future mission. I know that in the minds of many of your classmates . . ." — here Simeon looked pointedly at each of his students — ". . . there is doubt that anyone can take my place.

"But I have carefully looked into your hearts, your minds, your past lives, and your current levels of spiritual awareness — as you have given me permission to do."

Looking steadily at his students, he continued: "And I have found that Thomas and Sabella have attained the level of spiritual growth necessary to step into the position I have held for many, many years in these Halls of Wisdom. The transition won't be immediate, but it will come. After that time I will guide you from my new position on the Higher Council."

He smiled sweetly at Thomas and Sabella. "You will do a fine job!"

Simeon touched them at the point between the eyebrows and mentally sent each of them a few special, private words of blessing and instruction. Then he sent them back to where they had been sitting in meditation.

"Now, I believe you have another two hours remaining, to honor your intention of meditating for twelve hours. I will join you for the remainder of the time. Please pray for one another and especially for Thomas and Sabella. They had no warning about this change, and all of us need time to go within and allow the transition, which has come upon us all so suddenly, to integrate itself within us. Let us meditate together with joined hearts."

Those remaining two hours of meditation were the deepest meditation that *any* of them had ever experienced. Simeon softly chanted AUM-m-m-m at the twelve-hour point. One by one in silence they drifted away.

Thomas and Sabella, inwardly prompted by Simeon, did not leave.

Simeon stood and offered each of them a hand. "Come to my home, my dear children. I'll be moving out of it soon and will not be back. Let's have something to eat and converse a bit more."

Joyfully, Sabella and Thomas strolled, one on either side of Simeon, to his small home.

CHAPTER 36

⌐✏⌐

"The Blessed Lord said: 'That one who, full of faith and love, becomes fully absorbed in Me,
I regard as best attuned to My path to perfection.'"

— Bhagavad Gita 6:47

Each had visited Simeon's simple home a few times over the years, but never with anyone else. This was a rare moment.

All of Simeon's students were aware that he valued his privacy, though he always would try to see a student who might be in need of his advice or counseling.

They entered his living-dining-kitchen area and sat, as he indicated they should, at his round, hand-hewn redwood table. The table had been lovingly polished to a high sheen. It was a warm and comfortable room.

They remained silent while Simeon prepared them a light meal of fresh fruit, freshly made cheese and homemade crackers. Their drink was an herbal tea, the ingredients harvested from Simeon's small herb garden.

"Simeon," said Sabella, "What is in this tea? It is so delicious. You've served it to me before and I was hesitant to ask, but now. . . ." she tapered off, leaving the painful idea of Simeon's departure unspoken.

Gathering her courage she continued: "You say you are leaving us. I might never have a chance to ask you this again." She turned her head aside to hide her tears.

"Sabella, I will give you my secret herbal tea recipe before I go. But both of you listen to me carefully now. I am not going far away in distance or in time. And I will be able in certain ways to be *more* with you than I have been in the past — in your hearts and in your minds. If you really need me to be present with you physically, call me, and I'll come immediately."

Thomas felt he needed to change the subject, in order to ask a very important question. "Sir, how can our former classmates come to see us as their guides, taking your place? Won't they resent us?"

"Only if you give them reason to feel that way. You must earn their respect gradually. And before I leave, I will offer you both a few days of intensive classes on leadership skills. You are already talented in these skills, but I have a few important secrets to share with you."

The twinkle in Simeon's beautiful silver eyes assured them that he would not leave them unprepared for whatever was to come. And the promise that he would still be available to them at any time, either mentally or physically, was a great comfort indeed!

Simeon went on. "Most of your fellow students are moving on very soon, into other fields of postgraduate studies or into full-time occupations. You'll soon have a new group of younger students to work with."

Sabella could sense that their time with Simeon was growing shorter, and she felt she *must* ask him to clarify something before they parted.

"Simeon, why the *two* of us? Why not just Thomas alone? Or me alone? I'll admit it helps me to think that I will not be alone in facing this new phase of my life, but isn't it a bit unusual for two people to be appointed by their teacher to carry on in his place?"

"Sabella, Thomas, I do this through my own inner guidance and also after lengthy consultations with the Higher Council. There is a good reason for it, but . . ." — here he paused and gazed at both of them lovingly — ". . . it is something that you must discover for yourselves. And you will in good time." He lapsed into calm silence.

"Why won't you tell us, Sir?" Thomas asked. "What is the big secret? In order to do the job, are we each only half competent and in need of the other to fill in the gaps?"

Sabella felt embarrassed at Thomas's boldness; still, in her heart, she knew she had the same question.

Simeon only smiled. "Give it a little time. It will be worth the wait, my impatient children. It's time for you to be going home now. We'll meet again the day after tomorrow for a few days of private leadership training. Rest well. Much energy and inner strength will be needed for the days and weeks to come."

"Sir," Sabella said shyly. "The tea recipe?"

"Ah, yes, my famous 'Thyme-Travel' tea blend recipe! I'll tell it to you right now; no time like the present." They all laughed together and the tension among them was broken.

"Well, first you harvest the thyme at just the right time of day." More laughter. Simeon appreciated "thyme/time" puns too. "Then you add fresh mint, bronze fennel, some rose geranium, both the leaves and flowers. . . ."

Sabella quickly memorized the details of the recipe and thanked him profusely.

Simeon very seriously instructed her not to share it with anyone except Thomas — who, Simeon knew, wasn't all that interested in such details anyway. Enjoying the tea's delicious taste, Thomas was happy just to drink it and leave it at that.

It was time for them to leave — to put a close to this momentous day. Thomas and Sabella went their separate ways — no more thoughts or words for now. All that could come later. But their hearts were overflowing with love for Simeon, their dear friend and mentor, now and forever.

MORE FROM THE AUTHOR
AND A FRIEND

Perhaps you are wondering if Thomas and Sabella ever discovered whether or not they were each other's true soul mates — if Sabella *was* actually Sunitia, the long-sought other half of Thomas's soul?

Thomas wondered about it too, of course, and eventually found the answer. But he told me that he preferred not to reveal the answer to you (or to me) at this time, but rather to say the following in closing:

"You may think that you have just read the story of my life in Ascending Treta Yuga, and how I learned to time travel and what time traveling taught me. These were *my* specific experiences, it's true; but I want to be sure that you, the reader, understand that the tale of my long, long journey through many lives and my many wandering steps through time and space are very similar to *your* story, also. In essence, there is no other tale to tell.

"New adventures await us all as we pass through our remaining incarnations. Fresh new challenges and victories are sure to come, until that final victory, which is inevitable. The glorious destiny we have waiting — every one of us, without exception — will be fulfilled when we merge back into timelessness, formlessness, and oneness with all that is. It's not a matter of 'if.' It's only a question of 'when.'

"In a way, it's simply a matter of time. But remember that time is a part of *maya* or delusion. Everything we want is already here with us, in the Eternal Now, if we can but realize this sacred truth. 'Know the truth, and the truth will set you free!'

"Surely, it is better for you to focus on your *own* amazing tale of time travel through the yugas, and on how to find the shortcuts which will speed up the process.

"No matter how long it seems to take, please know that there is great *'joy in the journey'!* Do your best to learn your life's lessons quickly and have fun all along the way. Joy and blessings to us all."

THE END

Printed in Great Britain
by Amazon

46812905R00096